Rincon Hill
AND
South Park

Dedicated to wonderful friends
Oscar Lewis and Lawrence Clark Powell
who have done so much in preserving our
western historical heritage
and to Joan Quigley for her
significant encouragement

Rincon Hill and South Park

San Francisco's Early Fashionable Neighborhood

Albert Shumate

Windgate Press
Sausalito, California

ACKNOWLEDGEMENTS

I wish to express my gratitude to the many who have so kindly aided me in preparing this monograph. I am most grateful to Dick Dillon, a friend of many years for writing the foreword to this book, and to Linda and Wayne Bonnett, the book's publishers, for their cooperation and support. I am greatly indebted to Betty Gardiner for her valuable assistance and to Charles A. Fracchia for his useful suggestions.

The staff of the library of the California Historical Society, under its director Bruce Johnson, has been most considerate, as have Roger Jobson and Grace Baker of the Society of California Pioneers. I have received special aid from Gary Kurutz at the California State Library, Dr. Robert Chandler of the Wells Fargo Bank History Department, Peter Hanff of the Bancroft Library of the University of California at Berkeley, Ed Carpenter and Peter Blodgett at the Huntington Library in San Marino, California, James Delgado and Steve Haller of the San Francisco Maritime Museum; and I wish to express my gratitude and appreciation to them.

I have been fortunate to have been aided by some of the descendants of those who lived on Rincon Hill and in South Park— Paul Bearce, Richard Burke, Joseph A. Donohoe IV, Joseph A. Donohoe V, Barbara Donohoe Jostes, Edward Griffith, Mrs. Guy Helmke, Anne Adams Helms, Dixon Heise, Mrs. Albert Kok, Mrs. Philip Landis, Elizabeth Lent Gordon, Woodward Melone, Margery Foote Meyer, Virginia Peterson, Helen Wood Pope, Mr. and Mrs. David Potter, Harry Poett, Frederick Witzel, Palmer Wheaton. To all of them I am grateful.

Other descendants, now deceased, of Rincon Hill and South Park families rendered great help. I would like to acknowledge them for the generous assistance they gave me in this project: Farragat Ashe, Helen Ashton, Anson Blake, Henry Miller Bowles, Peder Sather Bruguiere, Mrs. Henry Carton, Angelica Hill Dunham, Ethel McAllister Grubb, Mary Greenleaf, Helen Weber Kennedy, Elliott McAllister, Mrs. Harold McKinnon, Emma Moffat McLaughlin, Mary Ingraham Edie Peeke, George Poultney, Betty Knight Smith and William Tevis.

Others who I should like to thank for their assistance are Lloyd Bainck, Sister Martin Barry, O.P., Dr. Gunther Barth, Raymond Black, George Brady, Dorothy Knight Carson, Mr. & Mrs. Jerry Cole, John Goodman, Frank Haylock, Lisa Jacobson, Dr. John Kemble, Joan and Ruth Quigley, Irene Neasham, Ruth Tieser and Robert Weinstein.

PHOTO ACKNOWLEDGEMENTS

Photo credits are given on page and in some cases are abbreviated as follows: *CHS* indicates the California Historical Society, San Francisco, California; *Bancroft* indicates courtesy, The Bancroft Library, Berkeley, California; *Huntington Library* indicates reproduced by permission of the Huntington Library, San Marino, California; *National Maritime Museum* indicates courtesy of the National Maritime Museum, San Francisco.

Library of Congress Cataloging-in-Publication Data

Shumate, Albert.
    Rincon Hill and South Park

    Includes bibliographies and index
    1. Rincon Hill (San Francisco, Calif.)— History
2. Rincon Hill (San Francisco, Calif.)— Description
3. South Park (San Francisco, Calif.)— History
4. South Park (San Francisco, Calif.)— Description
5. San Francisco (Calif.)— History.   6. San Francisco
(Calif.)— Description.   7. Architecture— California—
San Francisco.   I. Title.
F869.S36R567 1988   979.4'61   88—17228
ISBN 0—915269—08—2

SECOND PRINTING

Printed in the United States of America

Windgate Press
P.O. Box 1715 Sausalito, California 94966

Table of Contents

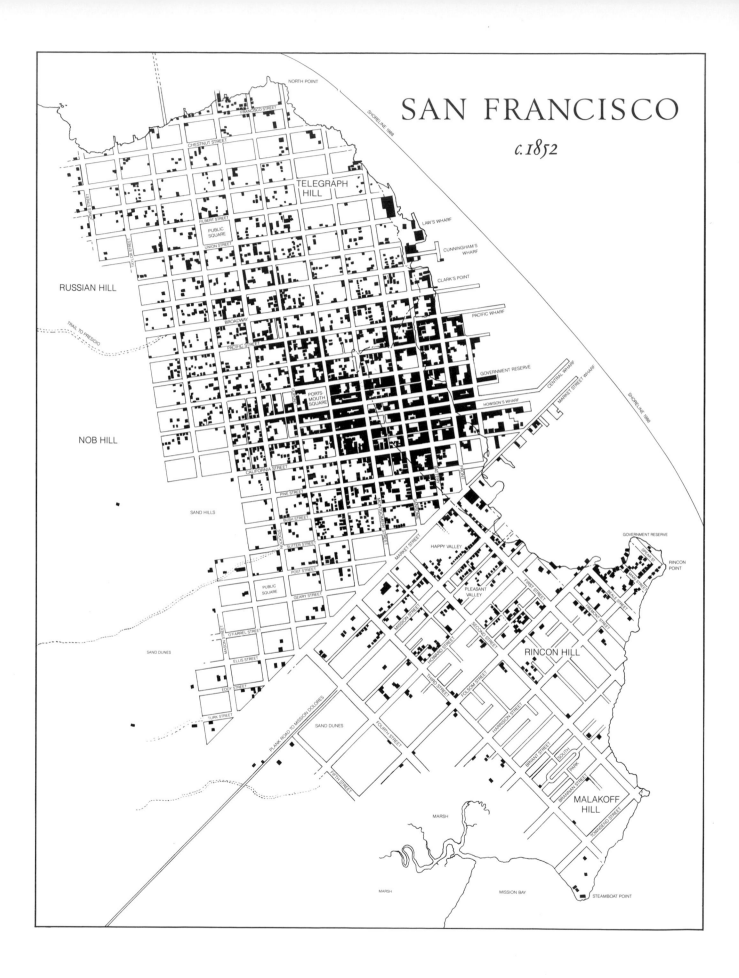

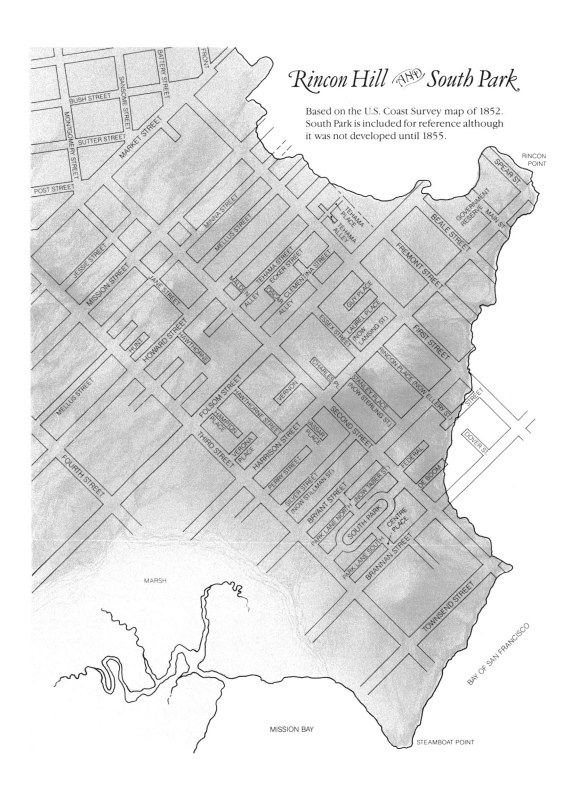

Rincon Hill *and* South Park

Based on the U.S. Coast Survey map of 1852.
South Park is included for reference although
it was not developed until 1855.

RINCON
POINT

BUSH STREET

BATTERY STREET

SANSOME STREET

FRONT

MONTGOMERY STREET

SUTTER STREET

MARKET STREET

POST STREET

SPEAR ST.

GOVERNMENT
RESERVE

MAIN ST

BEALE STREET

TEHAMA
PLACE

TEHAMA
ALLEY

FREMONT STREET

MINNA STREET

MELLUS STREET

JESSIE STREET

MISSION STREET

JANE STREET

MALDEN
ALLEY

TEHAMA STREET

ECKER STREET

OSCAR
ALLEY

CLEMENTINA STREET

GUY PLACE

LAUREL PLACE
(NOW
LANSING ST)

ESSEX STREET

FIRST STREET

HUNT

HOWARD STREET

HAWTHORNE

MELLUS STREET

CHARLES PL

RINCON PLACE (NOW ELLERY ST)

STANLEY PLACE
(NOW STERLING ST)

STREET

FOLSOM STREET

HAWTHORNE STREET

VERNON

HARRISON STREET

HAMPTON
PLACE

VERONA
PLACE

NASSAU
PLACE

SECOND STREET

DOVER ST.

THIRD STREET

PERRY STREET

SILVER STREET
(NOW STILLMAN ST)

BRYANT STREET

FEDERAL

DE BOOM

FOURTH STREET

PARK LANE NORTH
(NOW TABER ST)

SOUTH PARK

CENTRE
PLACE

PARK LANE SOUTH

BRANNAN STREET

MARSH

TOWNSEND STREET

BAY OF SAN FRANCISCO

MISSION BAY

STEAMBOAT POINT

A drawing by William Rich Hutton of the village of San Francisco, September 25, 1847, just before the discovery of gold. Yerba Buena Cove is not yet filled and extends to Montgomery Street. On the southern rim of the cove (right), Rincon Point and Rincon Hill are clearly shown.
Huntington Library

FOREWORD

Few poets have ever sung the glories of San Francisco's South of Market area. This is so although Charles Warren Stoddard, Henry George, Hubert H. Bancroft and Theodore Hittell all lived in the district; Jack London was born there; and Gertrude Atherton observed that its Rincon Hill and South Park were the only places in town "where one could be born respectably." Only Bret Harte, another resident, made the sector the subject of verse in his jocular elegy of 1864, "South Park."

Indeed, we have had to endure 138 years of patience, from first settlement, for an adequately-detailed history of this old quarter of the city. But the long wait has been worth it. The proverbial right man at the right time has come along in the person of Dr. Albert Shumate, whose succinct text, the result of several decades of research, is handsomely enhanced by a treasure trove of historic photographs. He does not neglect hospitals and schools, churches and philanthropic institutions but, rightly, his focus is on the pioneer gentry and their grand homes.

The sleepy and almost classless seaport of Yerba Buena of 1847 metamorphosed into an instant city and by the early 1850s was a metropolis, complete with a *nouveau riche* aristocracy. Often-told is the tale of the movers and shakers who made possible an "imperial" San Francisco that was to dominate economically the Pacific Coast. These men were symbolized by the Nobs, or Nabobs, of gold, silver, and railroads who scaled Nob Hill during the Gilded Age of the 1870s to build upon its summit. Their opulent mansions seemed to prove, in advance, Thorstein Veblen's 1899 theory of conspicuous consumption, often attributed to the newly rich by persons with less money but more discrimination.

Little known, till now, are the details of the earlier chapter of the story of San Francisco's baronial businessmen. As early as 1849 they accompanied ordinary Irish workingmen across Market Street to Happy Valley. Peter Donahue had just transferred there his pioneering Union Iron Works. This area, between Market Street and Mission Creek, was the city's "banana belt," sheltered from westerlies and fog banks by high Roman hills.

Donahue's presence brought not only his brother James and old pal and near-namesake Joe Donohoe ("The Honest Banker") to the slopes of Rincon Hill. It also attracted as neighbors his successors at the iron works and gas company, Irving Scott and William Bourn; his San Francisco and San Jose Railroad contractor, A.H. Houston; and his friend-yet-rival in railroading, Senator Milton Latham.

When Donahue built the San Francisco Gas Company in 1852 in Happy Valley, he used so many Hibernians from Ulster that the valley was briefly called "the Derry Reservation." Both names were soon replaced by a more lasting third one, Tar Flat. Before natural gas was tamed, illuminating gas for street lamps was made from coal. The by-product of coal tar was then useless, so Donahue just let it run into the mud flats. Hence the new name for Happy Valley, Tar Flat.

South of Market, or South of the Slot after cable cars began to run on Market Street, became as Irish as South Boston. Its Boston-like brogue, in fact, distinguished genuine "South of Market Boys" from the rest of the native born population until a wave of newcomers submerged this ethnic presence during and after World War II.

Even earlier Happy Valley settlers than businessmen or skilled workers were the Gold Rush era squatters who occupied choice parts of the old pastoral *potreros* of Mexican Yerba Buena. Their homes ranged downward from tents and shacks to wagon beds, beached boats, and even a large crockery hogshead. Old-timers still debate whether the name they gave to the green oasis of grass and live oaks beyond the sand hills was assigned in mockery. For the "fine springs" of early travelers turned out to be brackish seeps that were vectors of disease. Dysentery and assorted agues and fevers turned Happy Valley into a sickly place; this name for an area checkerboarded with small graveyards was perhaps sarcastic.

The squatters were forced out by the influx of such prominent and well-heeled entrepreneurs as Fremont, Lick, Folsom, Brannan, Larkin, and (W.D.M.) Howard. They not only built fine homes; they continued their speculating (second nature to them) by building rental cottages for the urban yeomanry mustering at foundries, shipyards, warehouses and machine shops of the locality.

As early as 1850, the city converted brush-clogged paths through the sand dunes into streets and, a year or two later, drove plank roads from the new homes and gardens out to Mission Dolores. But it was Peter Donahue who tied the South of Market area to the outside world. He first ran a line of omnibuses — trackless horse-drawn streetcars — from Happy Valley across town to Meiggs Wharf and North Beach. He then placed the terminal of his San Francisco and San Jose Railroad, the city's first railway, in his own neighborhood. Donahue intended it to be the first leg of a transcontinental railroad, but the Glaswegian was outfoxed by the Central Pacific's Big Four. Peter's Union Iron Works remained the major man-made landmark of the area until it was eclipsed in 1864 by the Baltimorean shot tower of yet another local resident, smelter owner and mayor Thomas Selby.

A half-century before Daniel Burnham presented his City Beautiful drawings to the supervisors, the South of Market area came up with the city's first real example of city planning. Sugar tycoon George Gordon hired architect George H. Goddard to design a residence complex along the lines of the squares, circles and crescents of London, Edinburgh and Bath. Goddard had been the designer of Holland Park in London. Gordon wanted his South Park, a dozen acres below Rincon Hill, between Bryant and Brannan and Second and Third Streets, to be the city's elite area. So he placed a ban on non-residential structures in his development, save for London-like mews, or stables, with coachmen's living quarters.

The tree shaded green oval was banked with thousands of fuchsias, geraniums and other ornamental plants. Until 1897 it was a private park, surrounded by an iron fence with a locked gate, much like New York's Gramercy Park. Residents were issued keys.

The very attractive garden subdivision proved to be only a limited success because its opening coincided with the economic depression of 1855. Still, important people chose to make their homes in its two and three-story English-style villas of brick, covered with stucco to simulate London's stone. They included Isaac Friedlander, the so-called Wheat King; Wells, Fargo's Lloyd Tevis and Louis McLane; the Big Four's "Fifth Man," David Colton; Robert Woodward, builder of Woodward's Gardens (direct ancestor of today's theme parks) and the temperance hotel, the What Cheer House.

South Park was adopted by foreign consuls, too, and by the local gentility. The very social Southerners included, besides Tevis and McLane, Senator William Gwin, General Albert Sidney Johnston, and Reverend William Scott. Scott was run out of town during the Civil War because of the Copperhead tone of his sermons and homilies but he later returned and in 1880 married Robert Louis Stevenson and his beloved Fanny. The presence of Johnston, a future Confederate general, was balanced by that of Henry W. Halleck, the attorney who built the fireproof quasi-skyscraper, the Montgomery (Monkey) Block, and who later became a Union Army general and Lincoln's Army chief of staff. As a downtown builder, Halleck had a rival in neighbor John Parrott, whose Parrott Building, of granite blocks from China, was carefully put together by coolies.

Rincon Hill, sliced off in 1933 to accommodate the San Francisco-Oakland Bay Bridge anchorage and approaches, was once the dominant natural feature between Market Street and the Bay. Well wooded with scrub oak and splashed with fall color (mostly poison oak), it entered tidewater as Rincon Point, to separate Yerba Buena Cove from South Beach and Mission Bay. Ironically, at the foot of this Parnassan height were clustered the shacks of China Camp, a fishing village so faithful to coastal Canton that Frederick A. Butman and other artists made it the subject of their canvasses. The Cantonese were the low men on the socio- economic totem pole and easy scapegoats during depressions. In 1877, violence spread across Market Street from Chinatown as an anti-Chinese throng, egged on by the rabble-rousing rhetoric of sandlot orator Denis Kearney, sought to burn the Pacific Mail docks and Oriental Warehouse. The mob was dispersed by William T. Coleman's last vigilante organization, the Pickhandle Brigade.

As early as 1860, South Park notwithstanding, Rincon Hill was the most fashionable and elegant address in town, the home of an elite that included Mizners and Maynards, Sathers and Stanfords. But in 1869, a state assemblyman and speculator, John Middleton, rammed the Second Street Cut through Rincon Hill in order to make South Beach more accessible, by easy grades, to Downtown. The steep-sided chasm, 87 feet deep under the costly ($90,000) and unlovely Harrison Street Bridge (Stoddard's "Bridge of Size"), was, in the words of Mayor Selby, "a public outrage."

Property values, instead of soaring as promised by Middleton, plummeted. A flight of the gentry to Nob Hill, luckily made accessible by Andrew Hallidie's new-fangled cable cars, ensued. Fewer and fewer South of Market addresses appeared in society blue books as the years rolled on. By the time that the San Andreas Fault decided to wipe the slate clean with seismic shocks and a firestorm, the district had deteriorated into one of run-down tenements likened to the "rookeries" of Chinatown by a Board of Health determined to condemn them. Mother Nature saved the Board the trouble in April of 1906.

Because of the cursed Second Street Cut, Dr. Shumate's story is, in part, a cautionary tale. It should warn us, once more, to remain ever vigilant, to be wary of forked-tongue politicians and their promise of "Progress."

Richard H. Dillon

Rincon Hill, 1860s

ARCHITECTURE OF RINCON HILL

Dr. Albert Shumate's collection of photographs illustrates clearly that the architecture of Rincon Hill in its heyday was a rich amalgam of former and contemporary styles. The preponderance of building before the earthquake and fire was residential, from the pre-fabricated houses of the early 1850s to the imposing mansions of the 1860s and 1870s. The Second Street Cut and the retreat of the elite to Nob Hill in the later 1870s, when the cable line made space more available to all the newly monied citizens, together signaled the effective end of Rincon Hill's prominence.

A few town planning ideas of admirable devising, like George Gordon's South Park, emulated private squares of Europe and the eastern United States. By and large, however, the inflexible grid plan of San Francisco, dictated by Jasper O'Farrell in 1847, precluded on Rincon Hill the romanticism and regularity of town design that London had experienced under the Prince Regent. Most wealthy Americans, particularly Western Americans, wanted individual houses, set on in-dividual plots of land, considerably varied in size if possible. The result everywhere in *nouveau riche* San Francisco, both in the later nineteenth and into the twentieth century, was infinite variety. The row houses of South Park with their modified Italianate character had their 1870s and 1880s counterparts in the endless wooden row houses of the Western Addition; but on Rincon Hill as later on Nob Hill, eclecticism was the rule, not the exception. Commercial architecture tended to be more functional, but even it bowed often to the caprice of fashion.

The single most important characteristic of Northern California architecture throughout the later nineteenth century was a preoccupation with tall forms of all kinds, whether in exterior practical and ornamental features or interior spaces, along with a persistent deviation from symmetry to asymmetry. Curiously, a fairly large number of houses on Rincon Hill were influenced by the later stages of Baroque Classicism or the Georgian style, with its strong emphasis on central focus, and by the earlier symmetric Italian Villa; they were four square and regular in shape, with strongly accentuated and balanced doors or windows. Classical columns quite often adorned porches of houses of this and later periods.

There was considerable overlapping of fashions and dates. Historic events such as the discoveries of gold and silver, and the early appearance of railroads in Northern California, were important factors. Most mid-century fashions began an average of five years later and continued five to ten years later than in the East and Midwest; Northern California fashions of the later century were more exactly contemporary with those of the East and Midwest, although here, too, there were some time lags. A kind of delayed eighteenth century architecture, with features of Baroque Classicism, often replaced the Classical Revivals of America's earlier nineteenth century. It was of relatively short duration (essentially in the early 1850s), and was modified by Gothic, and especially Italianate features.

Italianate architecture of Northern California produced only a few "villas" with centralized high massing; the actual tower of the Italian villa occasionally appeared off-center, with later Italianate or Classical details. The Italianate architecture of San Francisco was strongly oriented to Mannerist Italian forms of the sixteenth century. This resulted in an emphasis on elongated shapes such as tall slender columns or colonnettes, and tall rounded windows.

Second Empire, with its Mansard roof forms, was less overtly Baroque in Northern California and often added features of Stick Style and the Italianate. Stick Style had a late phase emphasizing pseudo-oriental or Moorish features (such as horseshoe arches) and elaborate turned wooden ornament of a "chalet" type, often termed Eastlake. These were uncommon on Rincon Hill.

Much other building presented an irregular effect; if fairly large, there were at least touches of asymmetry. One must not forget that the standard lot in San Francisco was twenty-five feet wide. This often necessitated, for modest residences, doors at the side of the front, not in the center, in order to make interior plans workable. Builders of more ambitious mansions often had several lots at their disposal and could plan as they wished. Some mansions even had gardens at the front or sides, on land that elsewhere in the Western Addition would be subdivided and built upon.

Dating these buildings, residential or commercial, is difficult. Some seemed precociously early for their stylistic character. Records are hard to reconcile with how buildings should look, if one follows a stringent sequence of changing architectural styles in the period. Dr. Shumate's work is essentially a history of personalities and their inter-relationships, of a lively era in San Francisco's history, and of a short-lived time of good luck and brash individualism when the great fortunes of the city were being founded. This is a history of the famous dynasties that were beginning their complex interweaving of the lives of men and women who had come from settled positions in the Midwest, South and East to establish themselves in a short time as financial and social leaders of San Francisco. It would be irrelevant and gratuitous to concern oneself unduly with precise dates or quibble over who built what when, in a vivacious era of expansion that paid little heed to architectural purity.

In the rich palimpsest of personality and rapid change of wealth and position, both up and down, which made Rincon Hill the pivot of San Francisco into the mid 1870s, one notes confrontations of the grand and the wretched: sumptuous mansions and elegant carriages on one hand; on the other, utilitarian buildings like the Sailor's Home and pedestrian pathways, dusty or muddy, through a virtually treeless landscape. There were a few carefully devised gardens here and there, but not at this early date before Golden Gate Park, any that resembled the grand parks and squares of Europe. It is curious that the veranda was an important feature on a number of the larger Rincon Hill houses, a Southern import which had been popularized in early Monterey and now appeared in diverse new stylish garbs. These early citizens seemed to glory in the noise and bustle of much of Rincon Hill.

One of the principal features of all residential San Francisco architecture was the bay window, appearing as an oriel type in the Gothic Revival and as a slant-sided bay in the Italianate and Mansard roofed houses of the 1860s and 1870s. It was a hall mark of more progressive commercial architecture as in the multiple bays of the Palace Hotel. One sub-architectural type that provided an amusing diversion of style in the city was the volunteer fire house. The special section of photographs in this work reveals that those on Rincon Hill were largely cast in forms of Baroque Classicism, with recessed parallel side doors and classicizing columns and projecting central sections. In this they echoed the strong impetus to this stylistic character in many of the more imposing residences.

Churches played an important part in the lives of people of Rincon Hill. One early example showed delayed late Georgian and Classical qualities, while St. Patrick's on Market Street, later moved and still standing, is a rare example of Provincial Classical Revival with Italianate touches. Most, as fitted the relatively short time of Rincon Hill's heyday from 1855 to 1875, were cast in forms of Gothic, popular throughout the country at that time and a perennial ecclesiastic building mode throughout the later nineteenth and earlier twentieth century.

Commercial architecture ranged from the penny practical gable roofed shed to the opulently stylish building in larger commercial concerns. San Francisco in the later nineteenth century, even more than most developing American cities, was in the throes of a truly violent and dramatic time of constant destruction and rebuilding. It was a major technological and structural period in world architectural history. Rincon Hill's golden or silver era was too early to witness the building of the steel framed ten or more storied structure; there were relatively few tall structures or kinds of visual skyscraper; one of these few was a tall, cylindrical structure, the Selby Shot Tower, used in the production of lead shot. Finally, in the later 1860s and early 1870s, grand hotels of multiple stories more palatial than any abroad appeared at the northern limits of the area. True highrises, however, were a phenomenon of the last years of the century.

Life on Rincon Hill must be relived through old photographs; only a few remnants of its past survive — and some of those that outlasted 1906 were destroyed later. In these photographs, collected and studied over a long time by the author, there is more explicit evidence of the world of architecture then than any treatise could detail.

In order to make the sequence of styles more systematic in the period from the 1850s to essentially the late 1870s or so, I include here a table of the principal fashions that flashed across the architectural horizons of Rincon Hill, with some supplemental notes to make them more precise.

Joseph A. Baird, Jr.

PRINCIPAL ARCHITECTURAL FASHIONS IN THE NINETEENTH CENTURY, PARTICULARLY THOSE RELEVANT TO RINCON HILL

The Classical Revivals
(*fairly uncommon in San Francisco*) — 1850–1855

Variant Forms of Baroque Classicism — 1850–1860

Victorian Gothic — 1850–1865
(and occasionally later)

Italianate — 1860–1875
(and later)

Second Empire, or Mansarded
(*Baroque Revival*) — 1870–1885

Later Victorian Gothic — 1875–1885

Stick Style or Bracketed
(*Eastlake*) — 1870–1885
(The above were most important for Rincon Hill)

Richardson Romanesque — 1885–1895

Shingle Style — 1890

Queen Anne — 1890–1900

Colonial Revival — 1895–1900
(None of these last made much mark on Rincon Hill)

N.B. Exact sequential arrangement of these dates causes some historical distortion; and dates are approximate but generally indicate earlier and later extent of fashions in Northern California.

INTRODUCTION

South Park! Rincon Hill! These are names that recall a once fashionable neighborhood of the early days of San Francisco.

In 1963 I became interested in this area when the late George Harding, who had been a president of the California Historical Society was leading a group of "Clampers" (members of the fraternal organization called E Clampus Vitus) on a visit to the site of what had been the most elegant district in San Francisco. Harding asked me to write a short account of the district's early days, a request that led me to write a monograph entitled *A Visit to Rincon Hill and South Park*, printed by Roger Levenson.

I became intrigued with the life of the man who in 1854 had created South Park, the Forty-Niner and innovative businessman George Gordon. The Gordon family had been the subject of two novels by Gertrude Atherton and had also appeared in her purportedly historical accounts of San Francisco. What she had written about the Gordons was pure fiction. That this prolific novelist, interested in dramatic story-telling, should have done so should not have surprised me.

In 1975 my biography of George Gordon, *The California of George Gordon*, was published. In this book, I stated that many of the statements that had been published about him were legends and nonsense. Nevertheless, articles still appear repeating these old fables, stories that appear to be more appealing than truthful. During the years since 1963, I have collected photographs of the charming residences that once graced South Park and the adjacent Rincon Hill, a hill now almost leveled. I have also had the pleasure of interviewing some ladies, who, as youngsters, had lived on Rincon Hill before the Earthquake and Fire of 1906. In addition, numerous descendants of the early residents of the area of South Park and Rincon Hill have been most kind and generous in providing me with information.

It has always amazed me how such attractive homes were built on Rincon Hill so soon after the discovery of gold in 1848. San Francisco was only a hamlet at that time; but, only three or four years after the gold discovery, during which time the hamlet became a bustling small city, elegant residences were being erected in what was consciously becoming a fashionable residential district.

The development of South Park and Rincon Hill presents an anomaly in the popular conception of San Francisco as an egalitarian boom-town in which the ways of life in those areas from which the argonauts came were set aside. This picture of a classless society developing in the *laissez-faire* Gold Rush San Francisco is not borne out by the evidence.

To begin with, although fortunes and comfortable incomes were generated by many who had lived in modest circumstances before coming to California, many who had come from wealthy or prestigious families continued lives of affluence and social eminence after their arrival. Even during the earliest days of the Gold Rush, when San Francisco was an undifferentiated mass of shacks and substantial buildings, of residences and working places cheek-by-jowl, and of retail and manufacturing in the same neighborhoods, Stockton Street stood out as a prestigious place for the wealthy and socially prominent to build their homes.

Soon thereafter, those whose money and family backgrounds demanded an enclave that indicated prestige built their homes on Rincon Hill. The development of the adjacent South Park in the mid-1850s was intended as an extension of this premier residential district. In the midst of a ramshackle, hurly-burly San Francisco, with its plethora of a *nouveau-riche*, largely male society, the residents of Rincon Hill and South Park were notable for the disproportionate numbers of families and for the large percentage of those who had come from politically, economically, and socially prominent families "back home." There had been a substantial number of families who had come from the Southern aristocracy, and who would form a body of Southern sympathizers before and during the Civil War.

These families, as well as most of those in the Rincon Hill and South Park area, introduced at a very early stage in San Francisco's development the traditions, institutions and customs of their places of origin. Houses were copied from the architectural designs popular in New England, the Middle Atlantic states, and the South. Gardens reflected the landscape designs prevalent in those areas. Charitable functions and social institutions such as balls and dances were like those remembered from home. Class distinctions and modes of behavior, such as dueling, were instantaneously adopted in the frontier city. Proper marriages within this class contrasted with the tendency of some newly-rich San Franciscans to take as wives women of easy virtue.

Hence, while the tendency is to view the San Francisco of the Gold Rush as a place of vigorous, classless life, as a brawling community of constant change, a close examination of the lives of the residents of South Park and Rincon Hill establishes a more complex life of the mid-nineteenth century American upper-middle class of the raw frontier city on the edge of the Pacific Ocean.

The South Park-Rincon Hill area did have numerous advantages: a fine view of the Bay, good weather, and proximity to business and manufacturing centers. Their homes, large and substantial though they were, were not ostentatious. As Kevin Starr wrote in *Americans and the California Dream*, "The tasteful elegance of Rincon Hill and South Park ceded to the garish ostentation of Nob Hill."[1] So, also, were the gardens of these homes noted for their beauty; and, even after the glory of Rincon Hill had passed, a newspaper in 1876 claimed that "the gardens of Rincon Hill are finer than those of Nob Hill."

Rincon Hill and South Park had become the homes of numerous leading citizens of San Francisco many years before Nob Hill became fashionable, and at a time when Van Ness Avenue and what is today known as Pacific Heights were still wilderness. And, even today, while newer families of San Francisco's establishment receive much publicity, the descendants of those who lived on Rincon Hill and South Park quietly continue to be an important part of this city's Society and of its business and financial sectors.

The decline of Rincon Hill as a fashionable residential area began with the "Second Street Cut" in 1869, a slicing away of the Hill along Second Street that was a tragic mistake. This ugly slash began the physical deterioration of Rincon Hill and ruined its beauty forever.

In 1873, Andrew Hallidie's cable car conquered the Clay Street hill, and shortly afterward the fashionable began their move to Nob Hill. In 1877, the *San Francisco Elite Directory* would refer to "Rincon Hill, where fragments of polite society still linger." By the time of the 1906 catastrophe little was left of the former splendor of Rincon Hill and South Park. The former homes of San Francisco's mighty were all destroyed by the fire.

The dean of writers on California history Oscar Lewis succinctly described the Rincon Hill and South Park of the 1850s: "They were then considered the city's most desirable areas. . . There the city's bankers, merchants, and other prosperous citizens built their homes; many were handsome structures, elegantly furnished in the style of the day. . . It was not until the 1870s . . . that South Park and Rincon Hill ceased to be the centers of wealth and fashion."[2]

That giant of critical literature about the west Lawrence Clark Powell wrote of the changes occurring in California, sentiments that also apply to the historical changes in the physical fabric of San Francisco: "California . . . has changed, is changing, will change and not always for the good. Old landscapes and seascapes become unrecognizable. Even the cities are not safe, as the sound of the bulldozer is heard in the land."[3]

Albert Shumate

[1] Kevin Starr; *Americans and the California Dream* (New York, 1973); p.354.

[2] Oscar Lewis; *San Francisco: Mission to Metropolis* (Berkeley; 1966); p.79.

[3] Lawrence Clark Powell; *Untarnished Gold, The Immutable Treasure* (Davis, Ca: 1970); p.16.

San Francisco from Telegraph Hill in 1854, from a drawing attributed to Alexander Edouart, showing the great changes in just a few years since the discovery of gold. Rincon Hill is in the distance. The large building in the center of the drawing is the U.S. Marine Hospital on Rincon Point; to the right on the crest of the hill are the homes of Church, Sather, Selby and Day. The church on lower part of the hill on the far right is Dr. Willey's Presbyterian Church on Natoma Street.
Bancroft Library

CHAPTER ONE

HAPPY VALLEY

In 1848, when gold was discovered, San Francisco's shoreline was quite different from that of the present. To the north were Clark's Point and Telegraph Hill, to the south Rincon Point and Rincon Hill. Between these two points, the Bay extended west in the cresent-like Yerba Buena Cove, reaching almost to Montgomery Street. South of the present Market Street, the Bay came to First Street—thus its name.

At that time, Rincon Hill was a real hill; while not as high as Telegraph, it did rise in certain areas to 120 feet, a sizable landmark. Because the hill has since been almost leveled, it is difficult now to realize that it was once a conspicuous feature of downtown San Francisco.

At the northwest foot of Rincon Hill was Happy Valley, extending along Mission Street from First Street almost to Third. In 1849, Enos Christman described the area: "[We] pitched our tent about a mile from the city. . . . It seems to derive its name from the merry character of its citizens who live in tents. . . . Several fine springs of excellent water are quite convenient and wood is obtained for cutting close by."[1]

Also in 1849, Rev. Samuel H. Willey wrote that the area was "refreshingly green and protected from ocean wind currents. . . . It was strikingly beautiful and in wonderful contrast with the desert-like sterility of the surrounding regions. It is not strange that it came to be called Happy Valley."[2] H. H. Bancroft in his *History of California* supports these descriptions, stating that Happy Valley was "sheltered from blustering west winds and provided with good water."[3]

George F. Kent, a New Englander from New Hampshire who sailed from Boston on the *Rodolph* and arrived in San Francisco waters on September 16, 1849, recorded in his journal:

> A part of the city well worthy of notice is "Happy Valley," so called—a large collection of tents pitched in a valley near the beach which may contain some 2,000 inhabitants, mostly newcomers waiting for a chance to go to the mines and miners who have left the digging for a season. These locate in Happy Valley wherever they see fit, and any attempt to collect rent of them (there have been several such attempts made) is rejected as absurd. This appears to be a regular "free soil" movement carried out into pretty effectual operation, for half a mile above there any piece of land large enough to pitch a decent sized tent on will rent for a very high price. In the Valley a variety of trades are carried on, and there are quite a number of shops for the sale of small articles, liquor etc.[4]

There were other descriptions of the makeshift shelters in Happy Valley: Forty-niner Samuel Upham reported that "the beach, Happy Valley, for the space of two miles is covered with canvas and rubber tents."[5] Charles Hotchkiss described some strange dwellings of these early times, one a "crockery hogshead" and another a "dry goods box."[6] Still another pioneer, Howard Gardiner, wrote that a covered wagon in Happy Valley was being used as a "homestead" and it "afforded excellent sleeping quarters."[7] Even ships were beached and used as dwellings.

But as early as October 1849, conditions in Happy Valley were becoming ill-fated, as the visiting Edward Lucatt, an English traveler, noted: "As he and I were taking a walk, we made a descent into a sandy hollow, bordering the sea, where much wretchedness and sickness were found under canvas tents, but which has received in mockery the name 'happy valley.'"[8]

Dr. J. D. B. Stillman provided another vivid description of Happy Valley in 1849: "The sandy shore of the bay is in front of us, and around us are sandhills covered with a low growth of evergreen oaks. . . . There are about one thousand men encamped along the beach." He did not report any illness then, but on his return in 1851 he noted that dysentery was killing the gold seekers, "caused by their reliance on hundreds of brackish little seep hole wells two to three feet deep,"[9] a shrewd observation for that time.

Even in 1850, the area was anything but "Happy," according to James Delavan, who wrote in that year:

> This Happy Valley became a scene of the most abject misery and distress. Disease was constantly abating the members crowded within it. . . . The water of San Francisco is not good, and very difficult to be obtained. Many have ascribed the virulence of the disease which has ravaged Happy Valley to the deleterious effects of the water and it is quite probable that such is the fact. [10]

T. A. Barry and B. A. Patten, in their well-known book *Men and Memories of San Francisco in the Spring of '50,* also recall that "Happy Valley was frequently a place of sepulture prior to the establishment of the Yerba Buena Cemetery" [11] (now the location of the Civic Center).

One of the victims buried in Happy Valley was Francis Forbes, Jr., son of the Chief Justice in Sydney, Australia. [12] Reacting to the reports of his death, some Australian newspapers attempted to stem the exodus from that country to California; the editor of the *People's Advocate,* for example, painted this grim picture of Happy Valley in 1850:

> The fever and ague, diarrhoea and dysentery had made dreadful havoc . . . and the awful pictures of the tent town or encamping ground at Happy Valley are horrifying in the extreme. To multitudes it has proven the valley of the shadow of death; and some of our informants, who went there by the *Inchinnan,* could with difficulty find enough of unoccupied ground to pitch a tent, the cleared surface presenting the appearance of numerous graves and forceably impressing on their downcast spirits that they had been thrown by their own voluntary exile into a Golgotha. . . . Many hundreds others were walking about the streets of the dreadful Happy Valley. [13]

Two physicians commented on the conditions in Happy Valley, both confirming the unhealthy state there. Dr. T. R. Palmer, the first City Physician of San Francisco, called Happy Valley the "most unhappy locality on God's earth;" while Dr. Hans Herman Behr, a medical graduate of the University of Berlin and for over fifty years a well-known resident of San Francisco, wrote that in 1851 he had noted a sign on Rincon Point reading "Cholera can be expected here," recalling the grim humor of the time. [14]

South of Happy Valley was Pleasant Valley, located between Howard and Folsom Streets and First and Second. It was graded and leveled very early. Henry Huntley, describing his visit to it in 1852, thought it was "strangely named, being a small, sandy valley between two sand hills, which deprive the residents there of all view." [15] He was visiting the home of Captain and Mrs. Ferdinand O. Wakeman, who had a "nicely laid out garden." [16]

Happy Valley was separated from the center of the city by a barrier of high sand hills. For example, Market Street, where the Palace Hotel now stands, had a sand hill 80 feet high. Bancroft wrote that South of Pine Street "high sand ridges [were] a barrier to traffic. The path skirted the ridge along the cove at the junction of Bush and Battery and entered into Happy Valley" [via First Street]. [17]

In December 1849, many leading citizens of San Francisco signed a petition urging the town council to provide better communication into Happy Valley. They claimed they had raised $5,000 to aid in opening Sansome to Bush Street, Bush to First, Mission to Fourth, etc. On January 18, 1850, the town council voted the sum of $6,000 to aid in opening these streets, including removing "the brush on the streets." The leading citizens who petitioned included many who owned land in Happy Valley, such as William D. M. Howard, Edwin Bryant, Rodman Price, Thomas Larkin, James Lick, and J. H. Poett.

These petitioners as well as other large landowners in Happy Valley, such as Captain Joseph Folsom and Sam Brannan, built homes there. Captain Folsom's elegant house, with its gabled roof and Gothic windows, was considered the first "mansion" to be built in the area.

Many of these pioneers built pre-fabricated houses which had been sent around the Horn or from China. In 1849, Bayard Taylor wrote that "Col. Fremont was residing in Happy Valley in a Chinese house, which had been erected on one of his lots." [18] In May 1850, Folsom was advertising twelve cottages for rent, each with eight rooms, a well, and an outhouse. William D. M. Howard also erected twelve cottages.

At the same time, the *Daily Alta California*, in May 1850, was noting "vast changes in Happy Valley," brought about by the appearance not only of houses, but of "machine shops, blacksmith shops and shipbuilding." The area changed rapidly. On February 7, 1851, the *Alta* observed: "In June and July 1849 tents were in Happy Valley. . . . Now large and elegant structures have been raised as by a fairy wand. Hills of sand have disappeared." Forty-niner Samuel Upham was amazed by the swift changes:

> San Francisco during my absence of two months had become so changed I scarcely recognized it. . . . I visited the gold diggers' encampment, Happy Valley, but that too was so changed I could hardly recognize a familiar spot. . . . A three-story warehouse was being erected on the spot where I had pitched my tent. . . .with no disrespect to Happy Valley there is one thing which, as a truthful historian, I am compelled, more in sorrow, than in anger to relate. The flea, that festive and lively little 'animile,' was quite prevalent. . . . The sojourners in Happy Valley and surrounding sand-hills never required cupping or leeching, as both operations were performed by the fleas *nolens volens.*[19]

The construction activities noted by Samuel Upham led the San Francisco *Herald* on April 10, 1851, to remark: "One by one the relics of San Francisco's early days are disappearing"—a statement sounding like a lament of more recent times!

Colonel James Ayres, writing in late 1853, described "Happy Valley, south of Market Street, and that valley and Rincon Hill beyond" as "pretty well covered with nice residences, some of the houses on the hill being of mansion-like dimensions."[20] Another visitor, C. M. Welles, wrote of this area in June 1854:

> A range of handsome private residences has been shown to me on Rincon Point, on both sides of the level and commodious plank road and surrounded with beautiful gardens, rich in verdure, whose site had been sand hills within three months; so rapid are the works of man and the operations of nature in this region of vivid life and tremendous energy.[21]

San Francisco in 1851.   Rincon Point is on the right.   *Author's Collection*

In the early 1850s, sand hills were leveled and the sand was dumped into Yerba Buena Cove and the swamps west of Third Street. The *Herald* on July 16, 1853, summed up the general opinion of this operation: "The Paddy [the Steam Paddy] is always the harbinger of improvement." This filling along the shoreline resulted in sales of water lots, that is, lots which would be filled and thus of potential value. The next year, for example, on October 26, 1854, the well-known auctioneers Selover and Sinton[22] sold parcels located in the Rincon Hill area bounded by Folsom, Harrison, Beale, and Steuart; by Harrison, Bryant, Beale, and Fremont; and by Bryant, Brannan, First and Fremont.

To serve the growing population of the area south of Market Street, public transportation was introduced in the early 1850s. In 1851, a plank-paved toll road was opened to Mission Dolores, starting at California Street and running on Kearny to Mission Street, then out Mission to the little settlement around Mission Dolores. In 1852, Folsom Street was planked and the swampy sections filled; this road also extended to the Mission.

That same year, omnibuses of the Yellow Line were in operation to the Mission, with a fare of fifty cents on weekdays and one dollar on weekends. These omnibuses were enlarged versions of the stagecoach, some holding eighteen passengers, and were drawn by two or four horses. Market Street, with its high sand hills, was not opened until later. A steam railroad went into operation on that street in 1860.

In 1855, the Yellow Line started service from South Park to the northern part of the city, running omnibuses from Townsend to Meiggs Wharf. Later, an opposition line, the Red Line, ran from South Beach to North Beach.[23]

In the early days of the city, fires were a constant danger to the flimsy wooden houses which prevailed. Between December 1849 and June 1851, six major fires had devastated San Francisco. To combat such disasters, volunteer fire companies were formed, including companies in the South of Market district. In 1855, the Tiger Engine Company, No 14, was organized, with a building on Second near Howard. In 1863, the South Park Hose was located on Third Street near Bryant. The following year, 1864, the Rincon Hose Company was stationed on Folsom Street near Beale. When the paid fire department was created in 1866, the volunteer system was abrogated, ending a colorful period.[24]

Describing San Francisco in 1852, *The Annals of San Francisco* records:

> There were other manufactories and workshops which were being constantly formed.
> In the district of Happy Valley particularly, which had been early selected for the site
> of such establishments,—there existed numerous flour mills and timber sawmills,
> iron foundries, marine and land steam-engine works, and steamer and other boat-
> building yards."[25]

A year later, June 9, 1853, the South of Market area was referred to by the *Alta* as "the manufacturing district of the city." Along First Street, in 1849, Peter Donahue had established the first iron works in the city, the famous Union Iron Works. Other iron foundries followed in 1850: the Pacific Iron Foundry of the Goddards, and the Sutter, established by George Gluyas and James Blair. George Gordon founded his Vulcan on First Street in 1851, and soon after came Daniel Hinckley's Fulton Foundry and the Palmers' Miners Foundry. The number of iron foundries indicates the importance at the time of meeting not only shipping needs, but also the great demand of the mines.

Conspicuous landmarks in Happy Valley included the Selby Shot Tower, built in 1864 at the corner of First and Howard Streets by Thomas Selby of the Selby Smelting Copany. The famous shot tower was 80 by 70 feet square and three stories (200 feet) high, looming far above the surrounding structures. It was used for the manufacture of shot, bullets, lead pipe, and so on.

Another well-known building was Union Hall, built in 1862 on the south side of Howard Street between Third and Fourth. The architect, S. C. Bugbee, designed Corinthian columns on the front, so it was first called Corinthian Hall, but as the Civil War was in progress, the more patriotic name Union Hall was soon applied. The ground floor housed streetcars, while above was a large hall 91 feet wide, 117 feet long, with a ceiling 31 feet high; it also included a gallery.

Events held in Union Hall's large auditorium reflected the changes occurring in the district: in November 1863, a ball honored the officers of the Tsar's visiting fleet; in August 1864, the Grand

Fair of the Ladies Christian Commission was held there; and in the early 1870s began the very fashionable Calico Balls. Union Hall was also the scene of action for mass meetings, such as the one held after Ralston's death in 1875. William C. Ralston, the banker and financier who had resided on Rincon Hill, has been called "the man who built San Francisco," and his energy and vision were such that one of his biographers titled his book, *Nothing Seemed Impossible.* One day after his removal from the Bank of California and its subsequent closing, Ralston went to Meiggs Wharf for his usual swim, during which he drowned. Some say he committed suicide. The mass meeting at Union Hall was called by his friends who denounced Ralston's treatment by the press and those who called his death suicide. The popular Ralston was a San Francisco hero, even in death. In the early 1880s Union Hall was a gathering place for the powerful Workingmen's Party. Finally Walter Morosco in 1885 converted it into a variety theatre (admission was ten and twenty cents).

Tar Flat was an early name for a particular section of the South of Market district. Unlike the names Happy Valley and Pleasant Valley, it did not disappear, but in fact became applied to a larger area. Originally, Tar Flat referred to the mud flats east of First Street. In 1852, Peter Donahue and his brother, James, built San Francisco's first gas works on First Street, a predecessor of the Pacific Gas and Electric Company. The waste coal tar from the plant was allowed to run into the shallow tidewater of the Bay, forming a tarry area to which the name Tar Flat was applied.

As years went by and the old Happy Valley region became a residential district of the working class, the term "Happy Valley" disappeared and the name "Tar Flat" was used in a broader manner to include this entire area. Kate Douglas Wiggin, for example, author of *Rebecca of Sunnybrook Farm* and other novels and director in 1878 of the Silver Street Kindergarten on Rincon Hill (the first free kindergarten west of the Rocky Mountains), referred to this South of Market section as "Tar Flat" and called it a "wretched slum."[26]

The deterioration of the Tar Flat district is evident in the action taken by San Francisco's Board of Health in 1896. At first, the Board ordered that hovels in Chinatown be demolished as health menaces, but then expanded their campaign to clean up the city. As the *Examiner* reported on September 17: "The Board of Health intends to destroy Tar Flat rookeries as well as those in Chinatown." The *San Francisco Chronicle* on October 29 listed the condemned rookeries—on Jessie, Stevenson, Clementina, and Natoma Streets.

The changes south of Market are reflected in a song of Tim Leary's at the end of the century:

> Dear old Tar Flat
> Sweet old Tar Flat
> That is where the Irish abound
> You will see some queer places
> And oft times familiar faces
> If you go there on the Howard Street car.

While South of Market was a workingman's district before the 1906 Fire, it was one full of vigor. For years, many leaders of the city were born there. The South of Market Boys organization long had happy reunions, and being born "South of the Slot" was an often-heard boast in City Hall. To quote Miles Overholt, a popular "poet" of the pre-Fire era:

> Whether you know your location or not
> The Heart of the City is south of the slot
> That is the spot
> True to a dot
> The Heart of the City is South of the Slot.

NOTES

[1] Enos Christman, *One Man's Gold* (New York, 1930, pp. 104-105.

[2] Rev. Samuel H. Willey, *History of the First Pastorate of the Howard Presbyterian Church* (San Francisco, 1900), p. 15.

[3] Hubert Howe Bancroft, *History of California,* Vol. VI (San Francisco: The History Company, 1888), p. 120.

[4] George F. Kent, "Life in California in 1849," *California Historical Society Quarterly,* vol. 20, no. 1 (March 1941), p. 29.

[5] Samuel C. Upham, *Scenes in El Dorado* (Philadelphia, 1878), p. 222.

[6] Charles F. Hotchkiss, *On the Ebb, A Few Log Lines from an Old Salt* (New Haven, 1878), p. 96

[7] Howard C. Gardiner, *In Pursuit of the Golden Dream* (Stroughton, Mass., 1970), p. 66.

[8] Edward Lucatt, *Roverings in the Pacific from 1837 to 1844,* Vol. I (London, 1851), p. 350.

[9] J. D. B. Stillman, *Seeking the Golden Fleece* (San Francisco, 1877), pp. 119-120; and "Diseases in California," *New York Journal of Medicine,* November 1851, pp. 290-292.

[10] James Delavan, *Notes on California and the Placers* (New York, 1850), p. 101.

[11] T. A. Barry and B. A. Patten, *Men and Memories of San Francisco in the Spring of '50* (San Francisco, 1873), p. 161.

[12] Jay Monaghan, *Australians and the Gold Rush* (Berkeley, Ca., 1966), pp. 57-58, 85.

[13] *Hobart Daily Courier,* March 20, 1850, reprinted from the *People's Advocate,* quoted in Monaghan, *Australians and the Gold Rush,* pp. 117-118. The barque *Inchinnan* sailed from Auckland, New Zealand, in July 1849 and arrived in San Francisco Bay on September 29, 1849.

[14] Henry Harris, M.D., *California's Medical Story* (San Francisco, 1932), pp. 58, 80, 387-389.

[15] Henry Huntley, *California: Its Gold and Its Inhabitants* (London, 1856), p. 20. A similar opinion was expressed by Elmer Munson Hunt in *The Gold Rush Diary of Moses Cogswell* (Concord, N.H., 1949), p. 46.

[16] Captain F. O. Wakeman's home was listed by the *Alta* on May 8, 1853, at Clementia and Ecker; later he lived at 402 Fremont. He was a member of the 1851 Committee of Vigilance.

[17] Bancroft, *History of California,* Vol. VI, p. 180. The Oriental Hotel, "fashion's first hotel," stood at the junction of Bush, Battery, and Market.

[18] Bayard Taylor, *Eldorado or Adventures in the Path of Empire* (New York, 1850), p. 208.

[19] Upham, *Scenes in El Dorado,* pp. 257-258. His complaint about the fleas became a constant lament of newcomers to San Francisco for the next one hundred years. Julian Brien, in 1903, wrote about the California Flea:

> "I'm a native son of California
> I live on the fat and lean of the Land
> I'm very much sought after
> Mostly after dark
> and am always Johnny on-the-sheet.
> I am waiting here for you."

[20] Col. James J. Ayres *Gold and Sunshine* (Boston, 1922), p. 128.

[21] C. M. Welles, *Three Years' Wandering of a Connecticut Yankee* (New York, 1859), pp. 265-266.

[22] Richard Sinton Arrived in San Francisco in 1847 on the U. S. warship *Ohio.* He served as Treasurer of San Francisco in 1851 and on the Board of Education, 1869-1870. In 1852 he was an organizer of E Clampus Vitus in San Francisco.

[23] James H. Leonard, *Through the Years with Muni* (San Francisco, 1976); *History of Public Transit in San Francisco 1850-1948* (San Francisco, 1948).

[24] Harry C. Pendleton, *History of the San Francisco Fire Department* (San Francisco, 1900), pp. 15-21. *City Directories of San Francisco.*

[25] *Annals of San Francisco,* 1852, p. 416.

[26] Kate Douglas Wiggin, *My Garden of Memory* (Boston and New York, 1923), pp. 110-118.

CHAPTER TWO

RINCON HILL

The Spanish word *"rincón"* appears in a Mexican land grant situated south of Rincon Hill—*Rancho Potrero Viejo y Rincón de las Salinas*—made to the Bernal family. Erwin G. Gudde, in his *California Place Names,* explains that *"rincón,"* used interchangeably with *"rinconada,"* means "an inside corner formed by hills, woods, or slopes. It was used for a projection extending into the sea, into the plains, or for a corner of land." Rincon Point was a true *"rincón"* until a part of the waterfront was filled in. [1]

In contrast to much of San Francisco, Rincon Hill was covered thickly with a growth of tangled shrubbery and small trees, "principally oak," to quote Dr. Willey. William Heath Davis, writing of San Francisco before the Gold Rush, told of hunting deer in the scrub oak on the south side of Rincon Hill. [2] There was also plenty of poison oak!

Early in the 1850s, wealthy pioneers began building homes, large for that time, on the crest of Rincon Hill. Three conspicuous residences put up before 1854 on Harrison Street near Second were the homes of Edward Church and Peder Sather, both bankers, and Thomas Selby, industrialist and a future mayor. A home prominent in the photographs of the early 1850s, on the southwest corner of Folsom and Second Street, belonged to Henry W. Halleck, an attorney who became Lincoln's Chief of Staff of the United States Army during the Civil War. Another early resident, General John Wilson, a cousin of President Zachary Taylor, built a home at Fremont and Harrison; while not as large as the above residences, it was noted for its lovely garden.

By the early 1860s, the *Alta* (February 4, 1861) described Rincon Hill as being "rapidly covered with elegant homes" and "unquestionably the most elegant part of the City"; a month later, on March 28, it referred to "the mansions of the wealthy on Rincon Hill and Point." Some of the residences built in the 1850s and 1860s that might be considered mansions included Peter Donahue's forty-room home at the corner of Bryant and Second (1860); Louis McLane's on Bryant near Second (1860); the homes of Joseph Donohoe (1862) and Millen Griffith (1859) on the 500 block of Harrison Street; and on Folsom between Second and Third, the residences of John Parrott (1854) and Senator Milton Latham (1864).

Evidence of the building boom on the Hill was a notice in the *Alta* on September 9, 1862, that W. H. Ladd was offering for sale eight homes on the south side of Folsom Street, between First and Second. All were two stories; the architect was George Bordwell and the contractor, John. E. Kincaid. On the north side of Folsom, between First and Second, were the homes for many years of the brothers-in-law Dr. Charles Keeney and banker William Alvord, a mayor of San Francisco. Other residents of Folsom Street were Horatio Livermore and William T. Sesnon.

Some noted persons who lived on Rincon Hill but whose homes are not pictured in this collection include General William Barnes, Mayor Henry Coon, and U. S. Senator Charles Felton on Laurel Place (now Lansing). On Essex lived Alfred Robinson and James Keene, who became the famous Wall Street speculator. On Beale Street lived the Fuller family (of Fuller paints) and Lansing Mizner, later a U. S. Consul to Central America and father of the "Many Mizners."

On Harrison, between Fremont and First, lived for a short time William Blanding (Father of Gordon), Adam Grant, Alfred Poett, and the Hamilton sisters, one of whom married Sir Sydney Hedley Waterlow, Lord Mayor of London. Hubert Bancroft lived on Harrison Street, while another historian, Theodore Hittell, resided on Folsom. Pierre Cornwall, after he moved from Sacramento to San Francisco, lived in the 600 block of Harrison, as did the industrialist Thomas Selby.

On Fremont Street were the residences of William Bourn, A. P. Stanford (brother of Leland), and A. L. Tubbs. Also living on Fremont Street (at 324) was William C. Ralston. When he left Rincon Hill for Nob Hill in 1871, his home became the residence of an associate of his, Asbury Harpending. It was here that the gems of the "Great Diamond Hoax" were examined. This famous episode in San Francisco's history began in 1871, when two alleged prospectors claimed they had found a diamond mine in a remote area in Wyoming. Harpending's enthusiastic reports resulted in wealthy associates such as Ralston, William Lent and David Colton investing in the venture. In 1873, Clarence King proved the mine a fraud. Harpending left his home immediately after the hoax was exposed. Some historians believe he was a participant in the deception.

On Bryant Street were found the residences of John T. Doyle and Henry Moffat, the cattleman, while on Rincon Place lived Leroy Nickel, Senior. Judge Orville Pratt lived on First Street.

Another small street on Rincon Hill was De Boom, named for Cornelius De Boom,[3] a consul for his native Belgium and associated with J. T. Townsend in real estate development in the area.[4] A resident of De Boom Street was the artist Juan B. Wandesforde, first president of the San Francisco Art Association.

Numerous marriages took place between the scions of the Rincon Hill elite. Prentiss Selby, for example, married his close neighbor Florence Church, and two marriages took place between members of the Joseph Donohoe and John Parrott families.

Some noted California authors lived on Rincon Hill at various times. An early dweller on Silver Street was Bret Harte. After the Second Street Cut, the ruined Sather mansion became the "eyrie" of Charles Warren Stoddard. It was there, in 1880 he met Robert Louis Stevenson, whom he introduced to the South Seas, to which Stevenson sailed eight years later to find his new home and final resting place.[5] Also, in 1880, Henry George completed his famous book, *Progress and Poverty,* in the former home of Cutler McAllister on First Street. A plaque marked this site until the building of the Bay Bridge. On Third Street near Brannan, another plaque, placed by the California Historical Society in 1953, marks the site of the birthplace of Jack London in 1876.

In the 1850s, on the south side of Rincon Hill below Bryant Street, there was a Chinese fishing village. *Chamber's Journal* of January 21, 1854, claimed there were "about one hundred and fifty inhabitants. . . engaged in fishing." A fine painting by Frederick A. Butman depicts this village.[6] On August 15, 1868, however, the *Alta* reported that South Beach had disappeared, including the Chinese fishing village. Photographs taken around that time verify that the entire area had been filled, much fill having been taken from nearby Malakoff Hill.

In 1863, during the Civil War, Rincon Point was seriously considered for gun emplacements as part of a defense plan for the harbor; but the *Alta* of October 2, 1863 reported that the batteries were to be finally located at Point San Jose (Fort Mason) and Angel Island instead of at Rincon Point.

By the late 1860s, South Beach had become the site of the Pacific Mail docks. The historic Pacific Mail Line, founded in 1848 before the Gold Rush by William Aspinwall, linked the Atlantic to the Pacific Ocean via Panama, the fastest route from the East Coast to California. After 1859, it confined its operations to the Pacific half. When the transcontinental railroad was completed in 1869, the Pacific Mail emphasized its service to the Orient, thus becoming the major carrier of Chinese to California.[7]

In the vicinity of the Pacific Mail docks, several large warehouses were built. The most noted, the Oriental, was erected in 1867 or 1868 and still remains, recalling the great activity of that area in the days of the Pacific Mail. A warehouse still standing on Spear near Harrison Street was built by Charles and Edmund Hathaway of South Park in the 1850s; it was a one-story building at first, but became a two-story warehouse in 1891. Another warehouse was Hooper's South End (1874) on Japan Street.[8]

Rincon Hill was the location for two of the largest structures in the city: the United States Marine Hospital (later the Sailors' Home) and St. Mary's Hospital, established by the Sisters of Mercy. The United States Marine Hospital was built on government land on Rincon Point (Harrison Street between Main and Beale).[9]

Incidents connected with the government's Rincon Hill land reflect the difficulty in obtaining a clear title to property in the early years. In 1849 that site, like other land in the city, was claimed by squatters. Some of the land had been leased for a limited time by Captain (later General) E. D.

Keyes to Theodore Shillaber, [10] who was unable to take possession because of the squatters' refusal to move. Captain Keyes acted as agent of the United States, by authority of General Bennett Riley, Commander of the United States Military in California. In October 1849, Keyes led troops to Rincon Hill to enforce the government's claim to this section of the Hill. Keyes evicted the squatters and demolished their tents and shanties. [11]

Besides the problem of squatters, several land claims in the 1850s clouded the title to land on Rincon Hill. One, the Sherrebeck, based on an 1837 Mexican land grant, claimed land from Rincon Point to the Mission; finally, in 1860, the courts refused confirmation. Another claim, the Santillan, plagued the landowners for years. Based on an alleged grant by Governor Pio Pico in 1846, it laid claim to 15,000 acres in the city. This "grant" was presented to the courts by the powerful pioneer firm of Bolton and Barron and was confirmed by the United States Land Commission in June 1855. However, the United States Supreme Court rejected it as fraudulent.

Lastly, the Limantour claim also affected property in the Rincon Hill area. J. Y. Limantour presented to the Land Commission his papers claiming much of San Francisco, including Rincon Hill. This claim was rejected in 1858, when it was discovered that the documents were forgeries, but not before many lot holders had bought title from Limantour.

In spite of the problems over obtaining title to the land, a contract to build the U. S. Marine Hospital on Rincon Hill was signed on November 13, 1851, but work was not commenced until a month later. As so often is the case at the present time, there were those who objected to the project. Certain property owners in the vicinity, as reported by the *Alta* in November 1852, called it "a great nuisance" and claimed it would endanger the health of residents in the area.

The building was completed in 1853 at a cost of $250,000, an enormous amount at that time. It was a four-story brick hospital, with beds for five hundred patients; if necessary, that number could be increased to seven hundred. It had protection against fire consisting of seven water tanks on the roof, two wells on the grounds, and two large cisterns. [12]

The earthquake of 1868, which centered on the Hayward Fault across the Bay, did considerable damage to some of the buildings in the central section of the city. Although damage was minimal to the hospital, the government declared it unsafe, and it was closed.

Several years later, on August 11, 1876, the building was leased at a rent of one dollar a year to the Ladies' Seaman's Friend Society for a Sailors' Home. (Similar Sailors' Homes were located in many seaports in the United States.) Prior to this, in the 1860s, the San Francisco Sailors' Home had been on Davis Street and later on Battery Street. The great earthquake of April 18, 1906, caused little damage to the building, but the Sailors' home moved from this location in 1912. In 1919, the venerable structure was demolished and a government building erected on its site. [13]

St. Mary's Hospital, another landmark on Rincon Hill, was located on Bryant Street at Rincon Place. After rendering service at the San Francisco City and County Hospital, the Sisters of Mercy, in 1857, had founded St. Mary's Hospital on Stockton Street near Broadway, the first Catholic hospital on the Pacific Coast. In 1860, the Sisters obtained the Bryant Street property on Rincon Hill, overlooking South Beach and the Bay. The hospital opened in 1861, and in 1872 a home for aged females was added, later known as Our Lady's Home for the Aged.

Again, there were those who objected to the building of St. Mary's. One who was not pleased, Casper T. Hopkins, a prominent insurance executive, wrote that in 1860 he had built a home on Rincon Place with a fine view of the Bay. Then "the huge St. Mary's Hospital commenced to rear its four-story walls," spoiling his view. In 1861, Hopkins leased this home to General Albert Sidney Johnston, who commanded the Army's Department of the Pacific. Only a year later, on April 6, 1862, Johnston was killed while leading his Confederate troops at the battle of Shiloh.

Incidentally, Hopkins also had difficulties with a neighbor on Rincon Place, A. H. Houston, a contractor for the San Francisco-San Jose Railroad. Hopkins complained that in defiance of a city ordinance, Houston kept "several hundred hogs . . . in the lot adjoining me to the windward." [14]

The earthquake of '06 did little damage to St. Mary's Hospital, but the fire that followed destroyed the building as the patients were being removed to Oakland by the ferryboat *Modoc.* Soon the hospital relocated in San Francisco, but Our Lady's Home for the Aged remained in Oakland. [15] For a short time on its return, St. Mary's was on Sutter Street near Divisadero. In 1911, the hospital was moved to its present location on Hayes and Stanyan Streets. But at the northeast corner of Bryant and Rincon Place, part of the old retaining wall of the hospital still stands. State Historical Plaque No. 84 on the wall recalls the site of St. Mary's and the former glory of Rincon Hill.

Several other hospitals were in the Rincon Hill area in the early days. The German Hospital, later called Franklin and now known as Ralph K. Davies Medical Center had its origin in 1854 on Mission Street between Second and Third. Later, in 1858 it moved to Brannan and Third Streets, where it burned on August 28, 1876. It then located on its present site, between Castro and Noe, Duboce and Fourteenth. French Hospital was for many years on Bryant Street between Fifth and Sixth. In 1895, it moved to its present location on Point Lobos Avenue (now Geary) between Fifth and Sixth Avenues. The short-lived British Government Hospital, established in 1852 and closed in 1860, was located on Main near Folsom. Another short-lived hospital was the Italian and Swiss Hospital on the southeast corner of Folsom and Third Streets.

Thus, all the leading European ethnic groups, the Irish, German, French, British, Italian, and Swiss, had their own hospitals in the Rincon Hill area for a period. Except for the U. S. Government Marine Hospital, these were the leading hospitals of that time.

NOTES

[1] Erwin G. Gudde, *California Place Names* (Berkeley, Ca., 1969), p. 269.

[2] William Heath Davis, *Seventy-five Years in California* (San Francisco, 1967), p. 134.

[3] DeBoom later attempted to develop a tract of land now known as St. Mary's Park. In that tract, a street was named Massily, the maiden name of DeBoom's wife.

[4] Many of the streets south of Market are named after builders of the first homes in that area, not only Townsend, but W. D. M. Howard, Captain Joseph L. Folsom, Edwin Bryant, and Sam Brannan. Mission Street recalls the old road from Yerba Buena to Mission Dolores.

[5] Albert Shumate, "Rincon or Telegraph Hill, Robert Louis Stevenson's Introduction to the South Seas," *California Historical Society Quarterly,* vol. 46, no. 3 (September 1967), pp. 223-234.

[6] This painting was a gift from Albert Bender to the California Historical Society. Frederick A. Butman also painted other versions of the scene. The *Overland Monthly,* July 1868, claimed that in his early career, Butman was the most popular artist in the city.

[7] James Hart, *A Companion to California* (New York, 1978), p. 318.

[8] The name "Japan Street" reminds us of the Far East trade of the Pacific Mail. Its name was changed during World War II to Colin P. Kelly, Jr. Street. Kelly, a war hero, dropped the first bomb to sink a Japanesse warship.

[9] C. V. Gillespie, *Abstract of Title—Government Reserve at Rincon Point* (San Francisco, 1865); and *Report of Attorney General,* 35th Congress, 2nd Session.

[10] Theodore Shillaber was a wealthy merchant at that time. Later, as Amelia A. Neville records, his wife had a weekly reception, which she called her "Salon."

[11] Frank Soule, John Gihon, and James Nisbet, *Annals of San Francisco, 1855,* p. 267.

[12] House of Representatives, 33rd Congress, Ex. Doc. No. 54, 1-11.

[13] After the 1934 waterfront strike, the Sailors' Union of the Pacific boycotted the Seaman's Institute and its Sailors' Home, and in July 1940, the Home closed. Rebecca Lambert, long connected with the Sailors' Home, arranged for a plot of land for the deceased seamen at the City Cemetery, located where Lincoln Park is now. She was buried there, and a monument long marked the location.

[14] Casper T. Hopkins, "The California Recollections," *California Historical Society Quarterly,* vol. 26, no. 3 (Sept. 1947), p. 260.

[15] Sister Mary Aurelia McArdle, *California's Pioneer Sister of Mercy, Mother M. Baptist Russell* (Fresno, Ca., 1954). Our Lady's Home in Oakland is now known as Mercy Retirement and Care Center.

CHAPTER THREE

SOUTH PARK

South Park was the creation of an Englishman, George Gordon, whose life in California was marked by extensive activity. In 1849, he had organized and led his Gordon's California Association from New York to the new El Dorado via the Nicaragua route. After arriving in San Francisco he became a lumber dealer and a builder of wharves; in 1851, he established on First Street one of San Francisco's earliest iron foundries, the Vulcan. The next year he built a block of iron buildings on Front Street. Four years later, in 1856, he founded California's first successful sugar refinery, an enterprise which brought him great wealth. His country home, Mayfield Grange, which was sold by his heirs to Leland Stanford in 1876, became Stanford's country estate and is now the site of the Stanford University School of Medicine.

The saga of the Gordon family was the basis of Gertrude Atherton's first novel *The Randolphs of Redwoods,* a sensation in 1883. She rewrote the story in 1899 as *A Daughter of the Vine,* again shocking San Francisco. These later "historical" accounts of the Gordon family contained much fiction. Gordon, for example, was portrayed as being a member of a wealthy Yorkshire family, a drinking companion of Branwell Bronte's, married to a barmaid, and so on. In reality, Gordon was born in London, never knew the Brontes, and did not marry a barmaid. In fact, his wife was the daughter of a draper and mercer of Market-Rasin, whose family owned a store in Lincoln from 1806 until recently. Incidentally, for reasons known only to him, Gordon had changed his name from George Cummings. [1]

In 1852, Gordon started purchasing lots between Bryant and Brannan and Second and Third Streets, an area described as "the only level spot of land free from sand in the city's limits." [2] Gordon's plan for this subdivision was outlined in an eight-page pamphlet, *Prospectus of South Park,* printed in 1854. [3] His object, as he explained, was to lay out "ornamental grounds and building lots on the plan of the London Squares, Ovals or Crescents or of St. John's Park or Union Square in New York, and equally elegant." Controls were to be exercised: "All stores or warehouses, saloons, etc., [were] strictly prohibited . . . [and the buildings used] exclusively for private dwellings." Further, he gave information on financing the purchase of the lots, including credit at 10% interest per annum.

The South Park subdivision was planned in four sections in the English crescent formation, the eastern and western sections being divided by Center Street. Tradesmen's deliveries were to be made by way of small streets in the rear, then known as Park Lane North and Park Lane South (later named Taber Place and Varney Street). Gordon optimistically predicted that the whole project, the entire four quarters, would be completed by the end of 1855.

Gordon's *Prospectus* also disclosed that "the architectural designs of South Park have been made by George H. Goddard, Esq., who was late architect to Lord Holland, and who laid out that magnificent addition to the West End of London, known as the Holland Park Estate." George Henry Goddard, born in 1817 in Bristol, arrived in California from England in 1850. He became a noted artist, surveyor, and map maker, as well as an architect. He died in 1906, and Mount Goddard, a Sierra peak, bears his name. [4]

Goddard himself described his work on South Park in a letter of April 30, 1854, to his brother Augustine in England:

> I have got a job laying out a large plot of ground for a square and ornamental garden with houses round for Villa residences a mile out of San Francisco, something in the mode of the new parts around London. My view of Lord Holland's Estate, Addison Gardens, procured me this work. [5]

By 1854, Gordon had obtained some twelve acres on the southwest side of Rincon Hill. He had acquired the parcels piecemeal, the major seller being James Blair, a member of the important Blair family of Maryland and Missouri. [6] As was so often the case in the early days of San Francisco, obtaining title to many of these lots involved difficult problems, since squatters often caused lengthy, costly litigation.

The prices paid by Gordon were recorded in his testimony in 1860 during the Rodman Price case. Gordon reported paying $3,000 for lots located at the southwest corner of Bryant bordering Third Street. Although records indicate that lot 106, consisting of the southeast section, sold for only $18,000, Gordon stated that he paid $22,500, but he may have added other costs, such as his expenditures on litigation. In any case, he testified that the lot had "no more intrinsic value than those for which I paid only three and five thousand dollars."[7] If we take Gordon's own figures, the six South Park parcels cost him a total of $48,500.

Three lots across Bryant Street, which were not in South Park proper but which Gordon bought, were lots 87, 86, and 85. He stated he paid $2,700 for lot 87 and $1,600 for one-half of lot 86.

On August 21, 1854, Gordon advertised in the San Francisco *Alta;* "It [South Park] is a convenient distance from the heart of the city affording a beautiful view."

The northwest section of South Park, the first to be built, was completed by the end of 1854. According to the *San Francisco Directory of 1856,* "the cost of this first quarter built on the northwest was $110,000." It also noted that "from the basement of each lot clay was taken sufficient to make bricks for the houses erected thereon. . . . The building provisions give almost perfect security against fire."

Most of the homes in this northwest section were two stories, with an English basement and similar floor plans. The basement contained the dining room, kitchen, servant rooms, and pantries. On the first floor were parlors, and on the second, bedrooms, usually five. In a separate building in the rear were stables and coachman's quarters. Exceptions to the two-story plan included Captain A. A. Ritchie's home at the northwest corner of Center and South Park, which was three stories.[8] The original deeds specified that houses were to be built of stone or brick. Actually, all these homes were built of brick and covered by a stucco that gave the appearance of stone.

On January 7, 1855, advertisements first appeared in the newspapers announcing a "Great Sale" of thirty-two building lots to be held on January 30. The lots varied from 97 to 137½ feet deep, with frontages of only 20½ to 29 feet. The *Alta* noted that seventeen houses had already been built facing south, that is, toward the Park.

A month after the sale, on February 4, the San Francisco *Herald* published an editorial entitled "Ornamenting the City—South Park":

> To George Gordon this city is indebted for one of the handsomest and most extensive
> improvements made during the past year. We allude to the laying out and ornament-
> ing of South Park and the seventeen elegant brick dwelling houses facing it.

The article referred to the homes as "mansions" and noted that "Third Street has been opened through the sand hills."

Development of the oval garden in the center of South Park began in 1854, and by December 25 the *Alta* could report that "the grounds are tastefully laid out; already about 1,000 young trees and shrubs are planted." In 1855, the *Alta* commented on the "floral beauties rarely or never seen outside of a private garden or conservatory" and the presence of "geraniums and fuchsias," two plants that are still popular in San Francisco. The *San Francisco Directory of 1856* described the oval garden as "75 feet wide and 550 feet long . . . laid out down the center of the block, surrounded by an ornamental iron railing." The residents of South Park had keys to the iron fence enclosing the private garden. Not until 1897 was it acquired by the city as a public park.

Many legends have circulated regarding this oval garden, one being that it was the same size and shape as the famed steamship, the *Great Eastern*; the building of the *Great Eastern,* however, was not started until South Park was about finished, and the steamer's size was larger. Also the park has been reported to be an exact copy of London's Berkeley Square; but their dimensions differ, Berkeley Square being 2.46 acres, and South Park only three quarters of an acre.

Gordon did not sell all the lots put up for sale on January 30, 1855, and continued offering them during the remainder of the year. A factor in the slowing of sales was the depression California suffered in 1855, the year South Park opened. Signs were evident in 1854 that the "flush years" of the Golden Era were coming to an end. No longer could a miner gain riches with his pick and pan. Placer mining was almost over as a means of abundant wealth. Deep quartz mining was in its infancy, and extensive hydraulic mining and dredging were still in the future. Disappointed miners were drifting into San Francisco to join the ranks of the unemployed.

In February 1855, the great banking house of Page, Bacon and Company closed after receiving the news of the suspension of its parent house in St. Louis. A few days later, on February 23, known as "Black Friday," Adams and Company, the banking house and largest express company in the West, closed after a "run." The panic that ensued led to the suspension of other San Francisco banks and a resulting depression that was to last for several years. During 1855 almost two hundred firms failed in San Francisco.

Gordon's lots sold slowly during these next few years, and he never made much profit on this venture. However, he continued to advertise his development during the remaining years of the 1850s. In June 1857, he offered lots for sale on Second and Bryant Streets, near South Park, and in February 1858, "lots with brick houses" were for sale in South Park.

The *San Francisco Newsletter,* April 10, 1858, reported: "George Gordon, esq., well-known capitalist of San Francisco, has let a contract for building 18 beautiful brick residences in South Park. They are uniform in style and will be finished in about nine months." Cobb and Sinton had some of these houses still for sale on July 24, 1860. [9]

On November 8, 1859, the first minute book of the Hibernia Savings and Loan Society (now Hibernia Bank) indicated how Gordon financed South Park. He asked for loans of $3,500 and $2,800 on his proposed houses, but the bank refused, offering him instead $3,000 on the first house and $2,500 on any of the other houses when finished.

The following January 7, 1860, the *San Francisco Daily Bulletin* reported on the "Progress of Permanent Improvements in San Francisco, new building at South Park and the neighborhoods":

> There has been a revival of work of improvement of South Park which has become
> one of the most desirable locations in the city. In continuation of the original plan
> George Gordon has erected seven fine brick buildings . . . [The] value of each is
> $4,000.

Also in 1860, Gordon was attempting to sell his own home in South Park, and John Middleton, real estate auctioneer, announced a "Great Sale" on October 22. He offered five unfinished houses on the south side of South Park and the entire northeastern quarter, which included seventeen lots between Center and Second Streets. The covenants of the South Park deed of trust prevailed as before; all were to be brick or stone houses used as private dwellings. In December, Gordon's ads were still attempting to sell unfinished houses.

By 1861, the advertisements emphasized new incentives for buying:

> The advent of the Bensley and Spring Valley Water Companies gives verdure all
> summer to the entire garden . . . a fine breathing place for families and children. . . .
> Mr. Gordon has arranged, we hear, with a company of Eastern mechanics whom the
> war has thrown out of work—masons, carpenters, and plasterers—who offer to erect
> this block at rate of wages but little over Eastern prices.

In December 1861, Gordon had for sale sixteen lots in the northeastern section, and in June 1862, the same lots were still for sale. On July 7, 1862, the *Alta* published an ad which read in part: "The location is not only eligible and healthful for private residences but has unobstructed views of the Bay, Alameda, and City and its surroundings."

Attempts were still being made in 1864 to dispose of the property. In one of Gordon's last ads, in the *San Francisco Newsletter* of July 23, 1864, he offered for sale lots on Brannan and on Second Streets and claimed he would close out at low prices, "as low as building lots in the sand filled swamps west of Third Street are selling at." The Gordon family left for a trip to Europe in 1865, but Maurice Dore Company held an auction in February of that year of lots #8 and #9 in the east section of South Park.

Unlike the northwest section, the eastern quarter was never completed as designed by the architect, George Goddard. As an example, Andrew Schrader's home built in 1869 was part brick, part wood. [10] His niece Mrs. Alfred McLaughlin (Emma Moffat), who was raised on Bryant Street behind South Park, told the author of the emergency plans her uncle had revealed to her: if there was an earthquake, he would run into the wooden part, if a fire, into the brick. [11] Another large home built on two lots in the 1870s at 11 South Park by Francis Berton, the Swiss and Portuguese Consul, was entirely of wood, as was the home of Celedonio Ortiz [12] at 7 South Park, which later became Senator Gwin's residence.

Although South Park was planned as an entirely residential area, a school was established in 1863 by Rev. Charles Miel, an Episcopal minister, who started a "Kindergarten" in the basement of his residence at 41 South Park. The next year he opened a school known as the Young Ladies' Seminary at #54-55 (later #55-56) South Park, in the southeast section; its exterior was fairly similar to that of the older residences. [13]

In 1866, Dr. Miel established a new school in Marin County, and the South Park school became Mrs. Bertha Zeitska's Institute for Young Ladies. [14] This school moved north of Market and relocated on Pine Street in 1878. Ten years later Mme. Zeitska returned to her native France, and her school became Miss Lake's, for years a fashionable institution.

When we consider that South Park homes were crowded onto approximately 21-foot frontages at a time when San Francisco still had so much open space, it may appear strange that the area became such a desirable location. One reason this came to pass was the wish of the residents to be some distance away from the central part of the city, with its gambling and drinking establishments, as well as brothels. Also, after the early disastrous fires, San Franciscans had a great fear of conflagrations, and South Park, removed from the main section of the city and built of brick, was considered less likely to burn. [15] Charles Caldwell Dobie expressed another factor in his book *San Francisco, A Pageant*: "It gave them [the residents] a sense of urbanity amid the sandhills which hemmed them in." [16]

Transportation also aided the development of South Park. As early as 1855, there was a horse-drawn omnibus on Third Street, which at first ran every thirty minutes, but later every ten minutes. This South Park to North Beach line was popular for many years.

Several livery stables were in business near South Park, the most prominent being George Poultney's. In the 1850s, his South Park Livery Stable was located on Brannan Street between Second and Third. In the 1860s, his stable (known at this time as Tattersall's) was at 342-344 Bryant Street; in the 1870s, it was opposite South Park, at 524 Third Street. [17]

To serve the area, many stores on Third Street used the name of South Park: the South Park Pharmacy, South Park Market, South Park Photographers Gallery, South Park House, and so on. In 1867, on the corner of Second and Bryant, a South Park Congregational Church was established, but it did not have a long existence, being one of the victims of the Second Street Cut.

In the 1850s, many prominent San Franciscans became residents of South Park. Among them were Robert B. Woodward, who would develop Woodward's Garden; Isaac Friedlander, the grain king; John Redington, with a wholesale drug business and quicksilver mines; Lloyd Tevis, later president of Wells Fargo; Charles De Ro, an auctioneer and later president of Gordon's Sugar Company; George Johnson (and his son Robert), a wealthy importer and Consul of Norway and Sweden; James Otis, a future mayor of San Francisco; William Lent, an affluent mining speculator; David Colton, who would be associated with the "Big Four" railroad builders; Rev. William Scott of Calvary Presbyterian Church and later founder of St. John's Presbyterian Church; Dr. Beverly Cole, who would become a president of the American Medical Association; George Wallace, secretary of Governor John Downey; and Isaac Davis, a lime and cement dealer. Davis later took into his firm Henry Cowell, whose fortune created the charitable foundation that bears his name.

It is also of interest that in the 1850s Southerners in San Francisco were a powerful group, both politically and socially. Many lived in South Park or nearby, including the William Gwins, the Hall and Cutler McAllisters, the Lafayette Maynards, the Louis McLanes, the Lloyd Tevises, General and Mrs. Albert Sidney Johnston, John Parrott, Reverend William Scott, Commodore James Watkins, A. J. Bowie, Jr., Dr. Beverly Cole, Dr. Richard Ashe, Milton Latham, Mrs. Thomas Selby, Mrs. I. Friedlander, Mrs. George Johnson, and Mrs. General John Wilson.

The 1860s found other well-known San Franciscans living in South Park: Horace Davis, banker and U. S. Congressman; Alexander Forbes, importer; the Hawley brothers, hardware merchants; Edmund and Charles Hathaway, wharf and warehouse owners; Charles Lux of Miller & Lux; James McDougall, U.S. Senator; Elisha McKinstry, Justice of the California Supreme Court; Christian Reis, banker; Asa Stanford, brother of Leland; Commodore James T. Watkins of the Pacific Mail; and Gregory Yale, mining attorney. [18]

While the area was becoming less desirable as an abode for the elite in the 1870s, nevertheless many leaders of San Francisco continued to live there. These included Senator William Gwin; Nicholas Gaxiola, Consul of El Salvador; Francis Berton, banker and Swiss Consul; Edwardo Cabrera, importer; Admiral David McDougal; Celedonio Ortiz, merchant; Andrew Shrader, San Francisco Supervisor; Vlademir Weletsky, Consul of Russia; Henry Williams of Williams, Dimond & Co., shipping; and George T. Bromley, "Uncle George" of the Bohemian Club.

In South Park's first year, 1855, an event occurred on November 26 that was characteristic of those boisterous early days. Many of the pioneers who had heeded the cry of "Gold!" and journeyed to California were natives of England, France, and Sardinia (Italians were referred to as Sardinians), and their countries were allied with Turkey in the Crimean War. The conflict centered in the Allied siege of the Russian city Sebastopol, guarded by the great stone Malakoff fortress. After months of fighting, the fortress and city fell in September 1855.

When the news finally reached San Francisco, festivities to hail the victory were planned in South Park, where a great tent was constructed. Two thousand enthusiastic men assembled to celebrate, and celebrate they did! The banquet's preparations were on a magnificent scale: "a bottle of claret at every place . . . champagne was plentifully supplied . . . hogsheads . . . contained beer." All went well at first, but in the second hour a row developed, according to the *San Francisco Chronicle*: "The wine and the excitement of the day were having their natural effect." For two hours the different nationalities sang their national songs and attempted to hang their own flags and pull down flags of other nations. There was "noise, confusion and strife. . . . The most hideous rowdyism ruled supreme." Thus this early attempt at international goodwill failed. [19]

That South Park and its vicinity had become an abode of the elite in the 1850s and 1860s was recognized by the city's first social register, the *Elite Dictionary of 1879,* in a commentary on the area: "There was little that was stylish and correct in the city except in its vicinity. . . . South Park became noted for its kettledrums, [20] balls, and Germans." [21] Wednesday was the accepted reception day for South Park and Rincon Hill. [22] Ned Greenway, the famous leader of San Francisco Cotillions, who once lived on Harrison Street, Rincon Hill, wrote in this flowery manner regarding the district: "We accepted only the few. . . . We lived aloof upon the Parnassus of the Golden Gate, the Sinai of the Golden Age. . . . It had once meant all that was great in the Western Social World." [23] Gertrude Atherton, born Gertrude Horn on Rincon Hill, made a similarly lofty observation: "Rincon Hill, South Park at its feet . . . two or three other streets near by . . . and Stockton Street . . .were the only places in those days where one could be born respectably." [24]

Still, all was not as perfect as the writers recalled in later years. In September 1865, an unidentified "South Park Lady" complained about the area in a letter to the *Alta California*:

> "[It is a] notorious fact that no lady in this part of the city can walk out after 8 o'clock
> alone, without being in danger of being insulted by ruffians and blackguards. Why is
> not the police force increased? Taxpayers have asked for them time and time again."

Shortly afterwards, on October 1, 1865, the Board of Supervisors suggested in a statement sounding like some current supervisors' wisdom, that more policemen should be hired, but their wages should be reduced to make that feasible!

After the Second Street Cut of 1869, South Park gradually lost its popularity with the elite. The *San Francisco Real Estate Circular* in September 1877 commented on its "faded gentility," noting that only "a few better class people still live there." It further advised that "the homes must come down for poorer but better paying property." The same publication in November 1881 repeated this opinion, observing that while South Park had been "intensely fashionable," it now was a "relic of bygone days" and should be replaced by "the best class of tenement dwellings."

The fate of Gregory Yale's home, located at the northeast corner of South Park and Third Street, is an example of the changes that occurred in the 1870s. After Yale's death in 1871, the property was sold to James Phelan, father of Senator James D. Phelan. He tore down Yale's home and erected a large frame apartment house on that site and the adjoining property.

By 1906, South Park had become a working-class neighborhood. A remark made by Mayor Jack Shelley at a St. Patrick's Day luncheon of the Serra Club reflects this change when he said he had been born on South Park in 1905 (just before the Fire)—the son of a longshoreman. To a certain extent, the story of South Park may fit the old saying, "Myth is much more enjoyable to relate than reality."

Poem by Bret Harte,
first printed in the *Californian,* September 24, 1864

SOUTH PARK
(San Francisco, California, 1864)
(After Gray)

The foundry tolls the knell of parting day,
　The weary clerk goes slowly home to tea,
The North Beach car rolls onward to the bay,
　And leaves the world to solitude and me.

Now fades the glimmering landscape on the sight,
　And through the Park a solemn hush prevails,
Save, in the distance, where some school-boy wight
　Rattles his hoop-stick on the iron rails;

Save, that from yonder jealous-guarded basement
　Some servant-maid vehement doth complain,
Of wicked youths who, playing near her casement,
　Project their footballs through her window-pane.

Can midnight lark or animated "bust"
　To these grave scenes bring mirth without alloy?
Can shrill street-boys proclaim their vocal trust
　In John, whose homeward march produces joy?

Alas! for them no organ-grinders play,
　Nor sportive monkey move their blinds genteel;
Approach and read, if thou canst read, the lay,
　Which these grave dwellings through their stones reveal:

"Here rests his fame, within yon ring of earth,
　A soul who strove to benefit mankind—
Of private fortune and of public worth,
　His trade—first man, then sugar he refined.

"Large was his bounty, and he made his mark;
　Read here his record free from stains or blots:
He gave the public all he had—his Park;
　He sold the public—all he asked—his lots!"

NOTES

[1] Albert Shumate, *The California of George Gordon* (Glendale, Ca., 1976), p. 49.

[2] Samuel Colville, *San Francisco Directory* (San Francisco, 1856), p. 205.

[3] This rare pamphlet, *Prospectus of South Park,* was located in the library of the University of California, Los Angeles.

[4] Albert Shumate, *Life of George Henry Goddard* (Berkeley, University of California, 1969).

[5] Letter located at the State Library, Sacramento, California.

[6] James Blair's father, Francis Blair, had been an important figure in national politics since President Andrew Jackson's term. James' brother Francis (Frank) served as a Congressman from Missouri and was later a U. S. Senator. He was a Civil War General. Another brother, Montgomery, served in President Lincoln's cabinet. James Blair died in San Francisco in 1852 while still a young man.

[7] *Rodman Price Trail,* 1862. "Deposition of George Gordon", pp. 238-261. Located at the University of California, Los Angeles.

[8] Archibald A. Ritchie was a sea captain who obtained several land grants in California, including the *Rancho Suisun* (17,755 acres) in Solano County, and the *Rachos Collayomi* (8,000 acres) and *Guenoc* (21,000 acres) in Napa and Lake Counties.

[9] John Middleton, *Auction Sale of Real Estate—October 22, 1860,* (San Francisco, 1860), a pamphlet.

[10] Andrew J. Shrader was a San Francisco Supervisor, 1865-1873. Shrader Street bears his name.

[11] This anecdote of Shrader's is also found in Louise Taber's *California's Gold Rush Days* (San Francisco, 1936), p. 39.

[12] Celedonio Ortiz, a native of Spain, was listed in the *City Directory* for many years as a capitalist. A daughter married Dario Orena.

[13] This school, also referred to as "The French and English Institute," had earlier been housed on Geary Street between Powell and Stockton. An institution with a similar name was at one time located on California Street.

[14] Also known as "Mme. Zeitska's French, German and English Institute for Young Ladies."

[15] These early disastrous fires and the subsequent rebuilding gave the city its symbol, the Phoenix, so appropriate after the 1906 holocaust.

[16] Charles Caldwell Dobie, *San Francisco, A Pageant* (New York, 1933), p. 233.

[17] George W. Poultney, a grandson, long interested in San Francisco's history, gave this author much information.

[18] Attorney Gregory Yale, a '49er and an authority on mining law, is said to have written the first book on mining laws published in the United States. He also served as the Master of California Lodge, No. 1, Knights Templars.

[19] Albert Shumate, "An Early Attempt at International Goodwill," *California Historical Society Quarterly,* vol. 50, no. 1 (March 1971), pp. 79-83.

[20] A "kettledrum," a popular form of entertainment in South Park, was an informal ladies' afternoon tea, deriving its name from India, where drumheads were used as tables.

[21] A "German" was a dancing party at which a cotillion was the main feature.

[22] *The Elite Directory* (San Francisco, 1879), p. 24.

[23] Edward M. Greenway, "The Golden Age," *San Francisco Call,* 1919. A "poem" summed up the career of Ned Greenway, long-time "King of the San Francisco Society":

> "He does not reign in Russian cold,
> Nor yet in far Cathay,
> But over the town he's come to hold
> An undisputed sway." etc.

[24] Gertrude Atherton, *Adventures of a Novelist* (New York, 1932), p. 4.

CHAPTER FOUR

CHURCHES, SCHOOLS, AND CHARITABLE INSTITUTIONS

Churches and schools were very early established to serve the residents of the Rincon Hill neighborhood. One of the first churches was Howard Presbyterian, founded by the Reverend Samuel H. Willey, who was preaching in Monterey, the old capital, when the Gold Rush started. Visiting San Francisco in the fall of 1849, he noted the tents in Happy Valley, and when he returned in 1850, he expressed amazement at the rapid changes that had occurred there: "A whole village of pretty cottages, ready made . . . had been put up."

Wm. D. M. Howard gave him a lot for a church on Howard Street, extending to Natoma between Second and Third. In 1850, Reverend Willey built a chapel; its plastered walls were a novelty in the new city, where almost all the buildings were lined with cotton cloth.[1] The church opened in 1851. In 1867, it was sold to the Third Baptist Society, a black congregation, and a large new edifice was erected on Mission Street near Third. For many years it had the largest Presbyterian congregation in the city. However, the neighborhood changed, and in 1896 the church moved to a "sandstone" edifice near the Panhandle, which it occupied until recently.

St. Patrick's was another early church to be established in the district. In 1850, there were only two Catholic churches in the area of what is now San Francisco: The Mission, a few miles from the Gold Rush city, and St. Francis in North Beach. In 1851, mass was first offered in a temporary St. Patrick's at Third and Jessie Streets. In 1854, a new wooden church was erected on Market Street where the Palace Hotel now stands. By 1868 as the congregation grew, the church building was no longer adequate. A new brick church was erected on Mission near Third Street and dedicated in 1872. Destroyed by the fire of 1906, it was rebuilt, using some of the old structure. It remains, standing alone in the new Yerba Buena Redevelopment District.

The old wooden St. Patrick's was not destroyed, but was moved to Eddy Street near Octavia and in 1873 was named St. John the Baptist Church. In 1891, it was again moved farther west on Eddy to a site near Scott Street and became the Church of the Holy Cross. In 1899, the present Holy Cross Church was built next to it and the old church used as a parish hall. It still stands, the oldest frame church bulding in San Francisco.[2]

The Howard Street Methodist Episcopal was also an important early church in the area. Organized in 1852, it had a building on Folsom Street by 1854. In 1862, property was acquired on the south side of Howard between First and Second Streets, and a substantial brick buildling was erected. In 1883, when it was flourishing, it was a very strict church, not approving of its members dancing or going to the theatre.[3] Destroyed by the fire of '06, this pioneer church was rebuilt on Howard near Sixth; the area had changed, however, and in 1927, it joined with other Methodist churches to build the William Taylor Hotel on McAllister and Leavenworth, which included the magnificent Temple Methodist Church. Unfortunately, the hotel and the church became victims of the Depression in 1937; the building continued under new ownership as the Empire Hotel until the Federal government purchased it. Now, it is part of the Hastings Law School.

A fourth church of importance, organized in 1858, was the Episcopal Church of the Advent. In 1860, a Gothic wooden church was built on Howard Street near Second, and consecrated in 1861. The Rev. Frances Marion McAllister was the first rector. His brothers, Hall and Cutler, lived on Rincon Hill and were wardens of the church; thus it was sometimes referred to as "the Church of the Holy McAllisters." The Howard Street site was sold in the early 1890s, and a new, larger brick building was built on Eleventh Street between Market and Mission. The disaster of '06 completely destroyed the church, but it later relocated on Fell between Gough and Franklin Streets where it still remains.[4]

Another Catholic church near Rincon Hill was St. Rose's, standing on the north side of Brannan between Third and Fourth Streets. From 1862 to 1878, it was a modest wooden chapel. In 1879, however, reflecting the large increase of Irish in the area, an impressive brick church was erected. Gutted by the fire of '06, it was rebuilt, retaining its old walls and towers. Since the parishioners did not return and the district was no longer residential but largely industrial, the church was closed in 1926; in 1940, it was demolished.

St. Rose's name continues, however, in St. Rose Academy. This school opened in 1862 next to the church, then in 1878 moved to the Western Addition on Tyler Street (now Golden Gate Avenue). The school building burned in 1893, and the school operated for a short time on two other sites. Finally, a few months before the '06 earthquake, it was located at Pine and Pierce Streets near St. Dominic's Church, where it remains.

St. Brendan's Catholic Church also reflects the changes in the Rincon Hill area as the Irish working-class families became a more and more dominant group. Established on Spear and Market as a chapel in 1879, it moved to the northeast corner of Fremont and Harrison in 1883. A wooden school was built next to the church, staffed by the Sisters of Mercy from their nearby St. Mary's Hospital. The school and church were burned by the fire of '06. After this disaster St. Brendan's continued on that location until 1913. Since 1932, the site has been occupied by the Apostleship of the Sea, caring for seamen and workers on the waterfront. St. Brendan's Catholic Church on Rockaway Avenue, near St. Francis Woods, was established in 1929 and is not considered a continuation of the Rincon Hill St. Brendan's.

The Catholic churches in the area during the last years of the nineteenth century were not the only indication of the large Irish working-class population; their "Halls" were another sign, such as the Hibernia Hall on Third near Folsom and the Irish-American Hall on Howard near Fourth.

In a photograph of the Rincon Hill area just before the destruction by the 1906 fire, Harrison Street is visible, and on the site of what was the Louis Garnett property at the northeast corner of Harrison and Essex is a new church, the First Finnish Evangelical Lutheran. It had previously been located on the first block of Mission Street and, in fact, was still there in 1905. This ill-fated Finnish Lutheran Church burned in the '06 holocaust, shortly after its erection. Even so, the church continued to use the site for its activities for a number of years.[5] The Scandinavian Lutheran Seaman's Mission was another group serving the many Scandinavian seamen in this area.

Schools also indicated the growth and development of the Happy Valley-Rincon Hill area. One of the first to be founded, in 1851, was the public school Happy Valley, located on Minna Street between First and Second. By 1854, however, it had moved north of Market to Bush Street near Montgomery. More lasting was the Rincon School, established in 1852 on First and Folsom Streets. Later, in 1854, it moved to a rented building on Hampton Place, off Folsom near Third.

In 1860, the School Department erected a two-story school building on Vassar Place, a small street off Harrison near Second. Still later, when a larger building was needed, a new school was built on Silver Street (now Stillman) between Second and Third. It will always be remembered as the school in which the noted educator John Swett taught.[6]

By 1860, the Rincon Primary School had over four hundred students and was one of the city's largest. The Rincon Grammar School, located nearby at Harrison and Fourth Streets also accommodated four hundred scholars.

The area also had several well-known private schools, including the Happy Valley Seminary for Young Ladies, opened in 1852 by a Mrs. Sanderson on Mellus Street (now Natoma).[7] In 1860, Mrs. Margaret Swedenstierna was head of the Collegiate Institute for Young Ladies, located on Third between Folsom and Harrison Streets. It later relocated at 64 Silver where Miss Margaret Lammond was principal from 1862 to 1866. She had earlier taught at Benicia. The Collegiate Institute's advertisement claimed it was established in 1855, when it was known as the San Francisco Female Institute.

One of the most popular schools was conducted by Miss C. B. Cheever in the second story of her family's stable at 24 Essex Street. Her father, Captain Henry A. Cheever, resided on Essex from 1856 until his death, and his widow and daughter continued to live there through the 1890s. Many children of the most prominent families on the Hill attended Miss Cheever's classes, including members of the Hooper, Merrill, and McLane families. Young Porter Garnett and Anson Blake were also pupils.[8] Alice Hooper McKee, a daughter of John Hooper, described Miss Cheever's "golden hair" and expressed the opinion of all when she wrote that "her pupils adored her."[9]

St. Patrick's Church conducted St. Patrick's School. As early as 1854, according to the *San Francisco Directory,* there were 250 scholars in attendance. Although no longer in existence, it served the area for over one hundred years.

Union College, described by the *Alta* (October 9, 1863) as "amongst the leading literary institutions of the State," moved to the southeast corner of Second and Bryant Streets (501 Second) in 1863. It had formerly been at 503 Dupont Street (Grant Avenue) and in 1860 had occupied Captain Folsom's old home at 236 Second for a short time.

At the time of the move to Second Street and for a number of years following, Union College was under the presidency of Dr. R. Townsend Huddart, a minister and well-known educator. As early as September 24, 1850, the *Alta* had published a "card" presenting his name for Superintendent of Public Instruction signed by such leading citizens as Joseph Folsom, Hall McAllister, Wm. D. M. Howard, and Alfred Robinson. Shortly after moving to the new site, the college added "a spacious Hall and Recitation Rooms." For many years it remained an important and popular school. By 1887, however, the area had changed so drastically that it merged with Boone's University School in Berkeley.

Besides churches, schools, and hospitals, numerous charitable institutions had their origins in this South of Market area. For example, the first two orphan asylums in San Francisco (and they may have been the first in California) were formed there. The San Francisco Protestant Orphan Asylum was established in February 1851 in a cottage in Happy Valley owned by Captain Wm. D. M. Howard. Soon a need for larger quarters developed, and in 1852 it moved to General Henry Halleck's spacious home at Second and Folsom, for which he charged only a dollar a year. A more suitable stone building was erected far out on Laguna and Haight Streets in 1854, and the orphanage remained there for many years. The present Edgewood Children's Center carries on the work of this pioneer institution.[10]

Shortly after the founding of the Protestant orphanage, a group of Catholic laymen met in March 1851, forming an association to establish a Roman Catholic Orphan Asylum.[11] These gentlemen included John Sullivan, D. J. Oliver, R. J. Tobin, and Eugene Casserly.[12] In 1852, at the urging of Bishop Joseph Sadoc Alemany (soon to be Archbishop), seven Sisters of Charity left Maryland for California to open the orphanage. Two Sisters died crossing the Isthmus of Panama; the remaining nuns were receiving the first orphans by September 1852. In 1853, a substantial brick building was erected on Market Street next to St. Patrick's Church, the present Palace Hotel site.[13]

The San Francisco Ladies' Protective and Relief Society, another major charitable group, was founded on August 4, 1853. In 1857, it was located on Tehama Street between Second and Third, Trenor Park's old residence.[14] By 1864, it had a fine building on the Hawes lot between Franklin, Geary, Van Ness and Post Streets where the Cathedral Hill Hotel (formerly Jack Tar Hotel) now stands. This Society merged in 1954 with the Crocker Old People's Home at Pine and Pierce to form Heritage House, a beautiful home for seniors on Laguna Street in the Marina, which opened in 1957. The Old People's Home had been formed in 1874 at Captain Charles Nelson's residence at 30 Laurel.

On the first block of Second Street during the 1860s was the House of Industry for "poor females." Members of the Board included Rincon Hill residents Mrs. Henry Halleck, Mrs. C. C. Keeney, Mrs. John Parrott, Mrs. A. J. Bowie, Jr., Mrs. Thomas Selby, and Mrs. William Ralston.

The San Francisco Lying-In Hospital and Foundling Asylum, also located south of Market, cared for "unprotected single women and their off-spring"[15]—in more modern terms, unwed mothers. For several years the asylum was on Jessie Street, but in 1877 it expanded to 762 Mission Street, near St. Patrick's Church. Attending physicians included Doctors Gibbons, Lane, Toland, and Cole, leading members of their profession. Some of the founders were Mrs. Henry Haight, Mrs. H. A.

Cheever, Mrs. Ira Rankin, Mrs. E. W. Church, and Mrs. Thomas Selby, all residents of Rincon Hill. The Asylum closed in 1893.

Three charitable homes under the auspices of the Diocese of California of the Episcopal Church began their work in the 1890s. The Sheltering Arms moved into a house at 579 Harrison Street in 1890, its stated objective to "rescue and reform." This home was supported financially by George Gibbs, a long-time resident of Harrison Street. The Mission of the Good Samaritan had its beginnings in 1894 on Second Street. This Mission has become the well-known Canon Kip Community House, which is still serving the needy in the South of Market area. A third Episcopalian charitable home was the Maria Kip Orphanage, named for Bishop Kip's mother and his wife, both "Marias". From 1890 to 1897, it was located at 570 Harrison, a house owned by General Lucius Allen; it moved north of Market after 1897. [16]

Changes in the district by the end of the century are reflected in the opening, in 1898, of the Co-operato at 645 Folsom, "a home for self-respecting women." For comfortable living quarters, each "guest" paid two dollars a week, which included board and lodging until such time as she could obtain a well-paying job.

Around the turn of the century, homes were torn down at the northeast corner of Center and South Park, and a large five-story building was erected, the South Park Settlement House. Aided by the generosity of Mrs. George Hearst, the Settlement House offered a haven for orphaned boys. Those living there had such activities as carpentry, printing, and baseball.

As can be seen from this listing, the South of Market area was the birthplace of many of San Francisco's important religious, educational, and charitable establishments.

NOTES

[1] Rev. Samuel A. Willey, *History of the First Pastorate of the Howard Presbyterian Church* (San Francisco, 1900), p. 40. Later, Rev. Willey was a founder of the College of California, which became the University of California in 1869.

[2] Luke M. Carrell, *Holy Cross Parish* (San Francisco, 1937).

[3] *The Retrospect, A Glance at Thirty Years of the History of Howard Street Methodist Episcopal Church, of San Francisco* (San Francisco, 1883).

[4] Rev. D. O. Kelley, *History of the Diocese of California* (San Francisco, 1915), pp. 343-344.

[5] E. M. Stensrud, *The Lutheran Church and California* (San Francisco, 1916), pp. 68-69; *San Francisco City Directory,* 1905; *San Francisco Block Book,* 1906.

[6] John Swett, *Public Education in California* (New York, 1911), pp. 105-135.

[7] *Alta California,* December 27, 1852.

[8] Anson Blake, "A San Francisco Boyhood," *California Historical Society Quarterly,* vol. 37, no. 3 (Sept. 1959), p. 217. Anson Blake, raised on Vernon Place off Second, served as President of both the California Historical Society and the Society of California Pioneers.

[9] Alice Hooper McKee, *Vignettes of Early San Francisco Homes and Gardens* (San Francisco 1935), p. 4.

[10] Nellie Stow, *The Story of the San Francisco Protestant Orphanage* (San Francisco, 1934); and *Edgewood Today* (San Francisco, 1966).

[11] *Report of the Trustees of the Roman Catholic Orphan Asylum* (San Francisco, 1857).

[12] John Sullivan was a member of the Murphy Party, 1843-1844, the first party of get their wagons over the Sierra. He gave the land for the sites of Old St. Mary's (the former Cathedral) and St. Patrick's Church. A son was a brother-in-law of Senator James Phelan. D. J. Oliver, generous donor to the California Catholic Church, especially the Sisters of Charity, was knighted by the Pope. Robert J. Tobin of the Hibernia Bank was a San Francisco Police commissioner for many years. Eugene Casserly became a U.S. Senator from California.

[13] Monsignor John T. Dwyer, *One Hundred Years an Orphan* (Fresno, Ca., 1955), pp. 12-19.

[14] Attorney Trenor Park, a native of Vermont, arrived in California in 1852 and returned East in 1864. Successful in dealing with mines, railroads, and the Pacific Mail, he retired to his native state worth many millions.

[15] C. K. Jenness, *The Charities of San Francisco* (San Francisco, 1894), p. 41.

[16] Kelley, *History of the Diocese of California,* pp. 114-115.

CHAPTER FIVE

THE SECOND STREET CUT

This was the most unkindest cut of all

—Charles Warren Stoddard quoting
Shakespeare's *Julius Caesar*

San Francisco since its earliest days had a determination to level its hills. Before the invention of the cable car or the advent of the automobile, popular opinion held that a level city would be easier to develop.

On September 29, 1853, Milo Hoadley was appointed Civil Engineer of San Francisco. He subsequently submitted a plan which called for the leveling of Telegraph and other hills. This plan met with opposition, however, especially from landowners who feared the lowering, raising, or moving of their buildings would be very expensive.

On April 3, 1854, the Common Council (as the Board of Supervisors was then called) decided that "because of sufficient manifestations of disapprobation on the part of the people," engineers would be employed "to investigate the system of grading." Appointed were J. G. Barnard, Brevet Major, U.S. Corps of Engineers; A. T. Arrowsmith, civil engineer; and James Allen Hardie, First Lieutenant, Third Artillery (the latter became a Major General in the Civil War). Their lengthy report, submitted on May 10, 1854, claimed that Hoadley's plan would result in the spending of millions to destroy the natural advantages of the hills and urged that the hills be preserved, but that some streets be graded. [1]

On May 22, an incensed Hoadley replied, denouncing their report and claiming that his was the "official plan." He further stated he had been aided by civil engineers William P. Humphreys and J. G. Hubbell. [2]

The outcome was that on July 7, 1854, the Common Council modified Hoadley's plan and the hills were not leveled. However, the grading that followed resulted in many peculiar "cuts." The San Francisco publication *Wide West,* on October 29, 1854, contained a humorous article about the "Gorges of Powell Street," including illustrations of homes left high above newly-graded streets. Other examples of "grading" included the First Congregational Church, located on the southeast corner of California and Dupont (now Grant Avenue) and, in 1853, probably the first brick church in San Francisco. After grading in 1855, its entrance was fourteen feet above the street level! In another case, Thomas Selby's home on Harrison Street was left perched high above the street when the graders were finished.

A lucrative business developed for those who had the machinery to raise and lower buildings. Newspapers for several years carried the advertisements of these contractors. Since grading projects continued, it is not surprising that on January 3, 1862, the *Alta* reported that "property owners on Rincon Hill are naturally very much excited" about contemplated changes in the grades on Second Street.

The following January 1, 1863, the *Alta* reviewed changes made in the preceding year:

> Nearly all the streets on the north side of Rincon Hill have either been cut through heavy banks or gently graded or filled in. The appearance of this portion of the City has been vastly improved since the first of January last.

But only a week later, January 8, the *Alta* warned San Franciscans:

> For twelve years we have had the leveling of hills, filling valleys. . . . The City was laid out by those who believe that there is no beauty in anything topographical but dead level, and streets running at right angles. . . . A wiser community would have tried to make their streets suit the topography of the site. . . . Even Telegraph Hill is beginning to disappear.

This warning was not heeded.

The next year, on September 21, 1864, the *Alta* forecast that a "little new town" would arise after Rincon Hill was cut down "south and west" of the Marine Hospital.

The infamous Second Street Cut was made in 1869, and the prime mover was John Middleton, one of the best-known pioneers. Arriving in San Francisco in 1849, he became one of its most conspicuous citizens. In the 1850s he was a member of almost every civic committee. As the *City Directory* described him, he was "not only the representative of the extensive business firm of Middleton and Co. but as a member of society we find him most prominent before the public."[3]

From 1861 to 1862, he lived at the southeast corner of Second and Bryant Streets (501 Second Street) in a large residence, which he later rented to Union College in 1863. Hittell, in his *History of the City of San Francisco,* explained Middleton's reasons for promoting the Second Street Cut:

> [Middleton] believed if Second Street were cut down through Rincon Hill to such a grade that heavy teams could pass over to the Pacific Mail wharfs, the southern end of Second would become a valuable business street. Thus he ran for the legislature and used his influence in having the bill pass authorizing the cut.[4]

As a Democrat from San Francisco, Middleton was elected to the 17th Session of the Legislature in the Democratic landslide of 1867, receiving 10,000 votes of the 17,000 cast. In the Assembly, on February 17, 1868, he introduced Assembly Bill #444, which authorized "the Board of Supervisors of the City and County of San Francisco to modify and change the grade of streets in said City and County."

This act "modified" the grade of Second Street between Howard and Bryant Street. At the crest of the hill, Harrison Street was to be lowered eighty-seven feet, and a wooden bridge was ordered built on Harrison across the chasm created. Also, stairs were to be built from the lowered Second Street to Harrison Street. The Supervisors were instructed to start work in thirty days. This act was passed by both State houses on March 30, 1868.[5]

In San Francisco, the tidings that the Rincon Hill Bill had passed were received with consternation by many. As early as February 18, the *Alta* had reported the introduction of the Middleton bill, and the following day a letter was published warning that the grading would be "unsightly" and urging that a tunnel be built instead.

On March 31, after the bill had passed, the *Alta* commented on the "confusion consequent to the insane struggles of the Senators . . . to modify the grade of Second Street" and expressed alarm about the possible outcome:

> The leading military chieftain of the State, the head of the Protestant clergy, the heaviest iron merchant [referring to General Halleck, Bishop Kip, and Peter Donahue] are but a few of the prominent gentlemen who will look down on residences, tottering on the brink of a precipice . . . May we never have to write their epitaphs, "How the mighty have fallen."
>
> A special meeting on the Second Street Cut was held April 19, 1868. J. B. Felton, a leading attorney, appeared for those opposing the bill. He claimed the Legislature's action was not compulsory, that the City "had official grades." It was stated that the "hill is the favorite place of residence of men of wealth" and that "many of the most elegant dwellings in San Francisco are there . . . The cut would destroy property," including Sather's $45,000 residence.

Another prominent attorney, Samuel Wilson, spoke in favor of the cut, asserting that the Legislature did have the right to order it, and that commerce on the waterfront and the "railroad terminus that is to be the Mission Cove" needed it. "Public opinion has declared that Second Street must be cut through," Wilson argued. Finally, he noted that the value of property had risen since the passage of the bill.

On April 24, 1868, the *Alta* published another protest:

"Many influential property owners object. They strenuously insist the Legislature's action is not mandatory, that they should not be compelled to abandon their property."

A few days later the paper reported another view, quite prevalent, which maintained that "a few influential people should not stop the march of improvement" and that "the interest of the entire community" was of greater importance. The April 1868 *Newsletter* proclaimed that "the destiny of San Francisco is clear . . . Your children will bless you" if the waterfront was filled from Mission Creek to the county line.

On April 28, the Board of Supervisors debated the problem. Dr. Beverly Cole approved the cut, alleging that property near the Pacific Mail would benefit; however, he did not object to "modification if thereby the beautiful residences of the Nabobs of the town could be preserved." Supervisor Charles Clayton asked to be excused, saying he was involved and would benefit. Supervisor Edward Nunan suggested that the whole bill should be "swept away." The final vote was six "Yes," two "No" and two abstentions, Clayton and Andrew Shrader. As seven votes were needed, the motion to approve the Second Street Cut lost.

However, there was no longer justification for further debate when the Supreme Court of California, in February 1869, ruled unanimously that the San Francisco Supervisors must "set about cutting down Second Street Hill"—as the *Real Estate Circular* expressed the Court's decision. The *Circular* article pointed out that the "earth and rock" would be used for "filling up swamp lots in South Beach and the Potrero," and concluded that the land would "be used for business purposes" and would "have a very beneficial effect . . . as it will give it a level path to the water front."

On February 24, 1869, the *Alta* commented that while Second Street was "doomed," all the "land in the neighborhood would be of added value." And on April 3, the newspaper proudly acclaimed:

"We have done more in a score of years in changing the topography of the city than Venice did in five centuries or Amsterdam in two, and those cities, like ours, were built up partly in defiance of nature."

On May 1, 1869, the *Alta* again expressed the opinion of many that "public necessity demanded that it [Second Street] be cut through." The same day, the *Newsletter* stated they expected the "retail business to move . . . to Montgomery Street South" and that property in the area "will be of great value."

Still, some doubts were being expressed. In July the *Alta* reported that "owners of property on Rincon Hill are certain to be pretty thoroughly fleeced by street contractors . . . property owners will be skinned, besides having their land rendered useless." And on July 31, in a letter to the editor of the *Alta,* a citizen wrote of being "amazed at the destruction of property" caused by the cut.

On December 6, 1869, the new mayor, Thomas Selby, who resided on Harrison Street, addressed the Board of Supervisors in these words:

Great judgement should be exercised in altering and regrading streets, or injustice and loss to many will be the result. Instances now exist when it amounts almost to confiscation. . . . Elegant homes have been destroyed under the plea of commercial necessity; and this in order that a few speculators might be benefited. The cut through Rincon Hill, with its bridge costing almost $90,000, is a public outrage—the result of special legislation—the baneful influence of which is destructive of legislative integrity.[6]

A century later, in 1968, Dr. Gunther Barth of the University of California explained the city's attitude:

They superimposed upon their unpromising hills a gridiron of streets that facilitated the sale and resale of lots in advance of actual settlement and thus assured their community the promotional benefits of real estate speculation. Their single-mindedness baffled apostles of organic growth whose country-like city streets would have followed the contours of the forty-two elevations that came to make up what Robert Louis Stevenson called San Francisco's "citied hills." Middleton's generation could see nothing objectionable in a project that decisively tackled another obstacle in the way of progress [Rincon Hill]. . . . Middleton's design appealed to many San Franciscans because it offered a partial solution to problems they had wrestled with for years. In the long view, the Second Street Cut would prove to be advantageous to all except the social elite.[7]

NOTES

[1] *Report of the Engineers upon City Grades* (San Francisco, May 12, 1854), a pamphlet.

[2] *Letter Published by the Common Council* (San Francisco, May 23, 1854), a pamphlet.

[3] A resume of some of Middleton's activities might read as follows:

1850 — Member, committee to celebrate California's admission into the Union as a state
1851 — Member, Board of Aldermen; trustee, State Marine Hospital
1852 — Director, Pacific Ice Company; marshal, St. Andrews Society, Funeral of Henry Clay Observance; member, Committee for the Relief of Sacramento Fire Victims
1853 — Member, committee for dinner in honor of Irish patriot, John Mitchell, on his escape from Australia to San Francisco; member, committee advocating a Pacific-Atlantic Railroad Meeting
1854 — Foreman, Grand Jury
1855 — Chairman, mass meeting trying to avert the failure of Page, Bacon & Company (Middleton lost $180,000 in this failure, according to Bancroft); President, California State Telegraph Company
1856 — Chairman of the ball at opening of the Lick Hotel; life member, California Lodge of Masons; Vice President of Sacramento, California, Pioneers
1858 — Member, committee of the Grand Celebration of Completion of the Atlantic Telegraph

Besides these many civic activities, Middleton was a leading auctioneer of real estate, the principal manner of selling property in the early years; his firm was Middleton and Co. He also was president of the Town of Menlo Park Homestead Associates.

[4] John Hittell, *History of the City of San Francisco* (San Francisco, 1878), p. 379.

[5] *San Francisco Municipal Reports* (San Francisco, 1870), p. 565; *Daily Alta California,* April 4, 1868.

[6] *San Francisco Municipal Reports* (San Francisco, 1870), p. 666.

[7] Gunther Barth, *Metropolism and Urban Elite in the Far West,* in *The Age of Industrialism,* ed., Frederic Jaher (New York, 1968), p. 165.

CHAPTER SIX

THE AFTERMATH OF THE SECOND STREET CUT
AND THE DECLINE OF RINCON HILL

Shortly after the Second Street Cut was completed, a "London Parson" (Rev. Harry Jones) visited San Francisco and then wrote about his experience of calling on the "Bishop of California" (Bishop Kip), who was listed in the *City Directory* as living "at 348 Second Street":

> [I] found in the part where his house ought to have been a fresh-made cliff, 50 feet high, on either side, and a crowd of navvies carting away stuff. It was impossible to reach the Bishop's nest from the street, so I beat round to get to the back of it. On arriving at the spot I asked where the Bishop lived. "The Bishop?" said a jolly-looking gentleman to me; "why, his house tumbled down into the street." [1]

Clearly, in 1870, the year following the cut, public disapproval became more evident. That year witnessed the election of not only a new mayor but many new supervisors. Six supervisors who had voted in favor of the cut no longer served, while two who had opposed the scheme, voting against it, were still members of the Board.

The *City Directory* of 1870 reported the Second Street Cut has "proved a more stupendous undertaking than was anticipated," employing 250 teams and 500 men on the project. The *Real Estate Circular* wrote early in 1870: "The cut through Second Street was made before the necessity for it existed"; later that same year the *Circular* noted:

> Before the cut was made the scheme had plenty of advocates, but now that it is made, not only does nobody want to pay for it but nearly all the property owners on Second Street claim they have been injured by it.

Contrary to the optimistic predictions that real estate values in the area would increase, the opposite proved to be the tendency. In October 1870, the *Real Estate Circular* announced that "one of the finest residences in the City, situated on Harrison between First and Second," was being sold. While the lot had cost $8,000 and the house $20,000 to build, it was sold for $20,000, the Circular stated, "because of the cutting down of Second Street and the certainty that all Rincon Hill will sooner or later follow it."

The residents of Rincon Hill started moving, as shown by the *Real Estate Circular* of December 1870, which reported the sale of two lovely homes on Harrison Street, one belonging to the William Lents and the other to the Charles Lows, both on the south side between First and Second.

This same publication in January 1872 commented on losses suffered by property owners:

> A sale was lately made on Second Street which strongly illustrates the injury done to many property owners by cutting down the hill. A two-story frame building on the east side, north of Harrison, costing $12,000 fifteen years ago, worth $20,000 to $30,000 when the cut was made, was moved back at a cost of $5,000 and sold for $5,000. The owners of the property . . . doubt the wisdom and incorruptibility of legislatures.

The controversy that developed over the house at 605 Harrison, near Second, also illustrates the extent of the losses faced by property owners. In 1865, Captain Fredrick W. Macondray had bought this house for his son Frederick, Junior, who had recently married Faxon Atherton's daughter, Elena. After the cut ruined his house, they brought suit against the city for $27,674.05, which they claimed was their loss after the auctioneer had sold it for $2,315.05.

The *California Mail Bag* of February 1872 reported similar difficulties: "Not a sale was made last year at advanced sales on First, Second, or Third Street," and on Third and Folsom a home had sold at a reduction.

Second Street between Market and Howard was another victim of the cut. When Market Street was still unpaved, this section of Second had many fine shops and was a favorite promenade of the of the fashionable. All of this changed after the cut, in contrast to the propitious, rosy predictions of the 1868 reports.

B. E. Lloyd in 1876, in his well-known book *Lights and Shades in San Francisco,* vividly described the results of the Cut:

> In the earlier history of San Francisco it was the most aristocratic residence locality. But then the Second Street cut was projected, dividing the hill into two half cones; its beauty was endangered and wealthy persons began to look in other directions for building sites, and the completion of the excavations has rendered it an undesirable place of abode. However some of the finest and most homelike private houses of the city stand on Rincon Hill. [2]

Historian John S. Hittell, writing nine years after the cut, reflected the changed opinions:

> The work was done, but the predicted benefits failed to make their appearance. The cut . . . has ugly steep banks, which have slid down in the weather. . . . Heavy teams have found it more convenient to pass through other streets in coming and going to and from the Pacific Mail wharf; Rincon Hill has lost much of its beauty and all of its pre-eminence as a district for fashionable dwellings; the most active advocates of the scheme made nothing by it, and direct expense of this improvement was three hundred and eighty thousand dollars, while the loss to the citizen beyond all benefits was not less than one million dollars. Many had to pay for the errors of judgement committed by a few. [3]

A question often asked is: How was this cut contrived when so many of the powerful, the elite, lived on the Hill and were personally involved? I believe, as has been shown, that there was a widespread opinion in the city that "progress" should not be hindered by a few and that the city in general would benefit.

Also, many had deep interest in the transcontinental railroad and concern about the location of the Bay Area terminus. During its early days, San Francisco had been a flourishing maritime city, supplying most of the Pacific Coast. Now a new age of transportation was arriving. Because of San Francisco's situation at the north end of a peninsula, there was fear that the railroad terminal might be located in Oakland or some other East Bay site. Thus the removal of Rincon Hill, or at least the cut, was supported because it would give access to level land from the approach to the city in the south, and would add more land for industrial expansion. Also it was believed the cut would provide a better road to the important Pacific Mail docks in South Beach.

Gunther Barth, in his study *Instant Cities,* comments on the urge for "progress" in the city:

> The logistics of transportation also finally pulled the railroad into San Francisco. The tribute the city paid for capturing the new advance in transportation seemed small. Rincon Hill was destroyed as the city's fashionable center. For the few who called the grading an act of vandalism, hundreds of others felt that the reckless attempt to accommodate the coming railroad marked them as advocates of progress. [4]

Still, "advocates of progress" can occasionally do inordinate harm to San Francisco. In earlier days, such schemes in the State Legislature as the Extension Bill in 1853 and another piece of knavery, the Bulkhead Bill in 1860, had been defeated (the Bulkhead Bill finally by veto of Governor John Downey). These defeats had occurred only because the press and most of the people united in opposition to the schemes. But such was not the case in 1868–1869.

During the same period as the cut, another scheme was being proposed by William Ralston and his cohorts: the extension of Montgomery Street, San Francisco's most important thoroughfare, across Market Street to the Bay at South Beach. Like the cut, there were those in favor of this extension. The *Alta* on January 6, 1869, argued:

> Montgomery Street can be extended. . . . The steep grades of Rincon Hill are but straw-like obstacles. . . .Though grading costs ten times what it does it will pay handsomely to remove the hill. . . . Owners of the lots will pay for the fill . . . and rock is better than sand.

Ralston showed his faith in the South of Market area by building the Palace Hotel at Market and New Montgomery, hoping it would be a magnet to lure business activities south. However, his New Montgomery Company formed for this purpose soon was two million dollars in debt, only one of the many unfortunate schemes leading to his empire's collapse.

This project failed, and New Montgomery never extended farther than Howard Street. The opposition of such homeowners as John Parrott and Milton Latham, who refused to sell, was a factor in its defeat. The *Real Estate Circular* in June 1872 related that the Montgomery Street-South scheme had been abandoned, and the same periodical in 1875, shortly before Ralston's downfall and tragic death, declared the New Montgomery Street project a "dead failure."

While general opinion was changing regarding the Second Street Cut, there were still those in favor of leveling the entire Hill. On March 21, 1870, Assemblyman E. A. Rockwell, a one-term Democrat from San Francisco, introduced a bill to level Rincon Hill. The *San Francisco Bulletin* on March 22, 1870, denounced this bill, stating it "would lead to bankruptcy of the city" and that it "is attempted to be rushed through the legislature . . . at the end of the session." Four days later, March 26, the *Bulletin* continued to argue against the bill:

> We can hardly believe the legislature will pass or the Governor approve a bill proposing to leveling Rincon Hill and filling forty acres of tideland outside of it [Mission Bay area]. . . . It is backed by a formidable real estate and moneyed interest. [We cannot] overlook the trouble forced on Rincon Hill property owners by reckless schemes. [This great expenditure was not] for the benefit of the community at large . . . but for . . . speculators. It will be observed that the expense of the Second Street cut which the City resisted as long as it could . . . works for the benefit of local owners and their benefit alone, and is saddled upon the public.

The *Alta,* however, did not agree with the *Bulletin.* On March 20, it urged the leveling of Rincon as well as Malakoff Hill,[5] and on March 28, repeated its appeal: "We must admit the necessity of removing Rincon Hill."

The *City Directory* of 1871 recorded that on April 3, 1870, there was a large gathering of citizens in favor of cutting down the Hill. The *Alta* of April 4, 1870, reported that this meeting was held in Union Hall and that attorney Henry B. Janes, who spoke in favor of the leveling, had been elected chairman. The newspaper also commented that the audience, composed mostly of "working class men," inquired if Chinese labor would be used in the undertaking and were reassured that "only whites" would be employed. However, the plans to level Rincon Hill did not materialize at that time; people had become tired of the many proposals for so-called "improvements."

The anti-Chinese viewpoint evident in this April 3 meeting reached its peak during the last years of the 1870s, a time of great depression. The boom years of the Comstock Lode were over, and the opening of the transcontinental railroad did not bring riches, but, in fact, brought cheaper Eastern goods to California. Moreover, Ralston's failure did not help matters. Agitators harangued the unemployed at the sand lots near City Hall, blaming the Chinese for all the difficulties. The "Sandlotters" believed in the slogan "The Chinese must go!" One of the objects of their wrath was the Pacific Mail Company, which brought the Chinese to California on its ships.

In July 1877, Sandlotters started burning Chinese laundries and attempted to burn Chinatown. Alarmed civic leaders called on William T. Coleman, the old "Lion of the Vigilantes," to head a Committee of Public Safety, including a Pickhandle Brigade. The mob, bent on destroying the Pacific Mail docks, was met by the police and the Pickhandle Brigade, who battled them on Rincon Hill. While nearby lumber yards were set on fire, the docks were saved; finally the rioters fled, and for the moment peace prevailed.

The Second Street Cut during these years became the hangout of young hoodlums whose brutal pleasure was to stone Chinese traveling by carts from the Pacific Mail docks to Chinatown. This was called "Rocking the Chinks," and the cut was referred to as "Apache Pass," a reference to that dangerous pass in Arizona. No wonder Charles Warren Stoddard about this time wrote that "at night it was dangerous to pass that way [through the cut] without a revolver in one's hand."[6]

After the cut, noticeable changes began to appear in the development of different sections of the city. In August 1873, the *Real Estate Circular* noted a basic movement: "Five Years ago the population and improvements tended Missionward; the last two or three years the current has changed and population and dwellings both set westward." This movement led to the rapid building of the Western Addition in the 1870s and 1880s.

Also, the 1870s saw the great mansions being erected on Nob Hill, the new abode of the elite. The building on Nob Hill had been facilitated by Andrew Hallidie's invention of the cable car and its conquest in 1873 of Nob Hill, previously called the Clay Street Hill and, earlier, Fern Hill.

However, the decline of Rincon Hill did not end the building of large homes on its crest. After the cut, for example, Henry Miller, the cattle king, tore down the brick Raymond-Earle residence at Essex and Harrison Streets and built a mansion. Across the street from his residence, at 507 Harrison, Irving Scott, president of Union Iron Works, also built a large house, which included what is alleged to be the first private art gallery in the city.

San Francisco's first *Elite Directory,* published in 1879, refers to Rincon Hill as the district "where fragments of polite society still linger." In the "calling and address section" of the *Directory,* eighty-three names are listed in the area, seventeen of whom resided in South Park.

Ten years later, in 1889, the San Francisco *Blue Book* listed thirty-seven entries from Rincon Hill, of whom only three lived in South Park, and of the three only the Edmund Hathaways were "old-timers." Nathan Masten was another long-time resident of South Park. A few of the early residents still living on Rincon Hill, on Harrison between Second and First, were the Baroness von Shroeder, Jerome Lincoln, Irving Scott, George Hooper, Millen Griffith, the Gen. Lucius Allens, and Joseph Donohoe. Also still on the Hill were Mrs. Peter Donahue, John Parrott, and U.S. Senator Francis Newlands who resided in the former Latham house.

In 1899, changes were even more marked: only twelve names were listed in the *Blue Book* of that year, including the Lincolns, Scotts, Griffiths, and Millers. One family listed was the Kentfields (Edward, George, and John), who had resided at 333 Fremont since 1859. Only the Griffith family had lived as long on the Hill.

Through these years, the decline of Rincon Hill was commented on by many. In the August 30, 1884 issue of a local magazine, *Ingleside,* a long article appeared bemoaning the fate of Rincon Hill and concluding:

> I wonder if the Second Street Cut ever repaid the incalculable damages done to this portion of the city? What a piece of chicanery the whole affair was, to be sure, and what injury did it work for the prospects of Rincon Hill.

A few years later, in 1892, Robert Louis Stevenson wrote of his impressions when he had roamed around Rincon Hill in 1880:

> I had discovered a new slum, a place of precarious sandy cliffs, deep sandy cuttings, solitary ancient houses and butt ends of streets. It was already environed. . . . The city, upon all sides of it, was tightly packed and growled with traffic.[7]

Stevenson's friend Charles Warren Stoddard wrote in 1902 of his abode on Rincon Hill, where he lived in "the Banker's Gothic" home (Peter Sather's ruined mansion) and claimed it had been "spoiled by bloodless speculators." Stoddard described the Harrison Street bridge as "the most unlovely object in the city," and complained that "the gutting of this hill . . . ruined the hill forever." "How the mighty have fallen," he concluded.[8]

In the 1880s or 1890s, a noted Bohemian Club member, Dr. H. H. Behr, previously quoted, delivered a humorous speech to the Club which reflected the opinion of that time.

> It was in the year A.D. 1868, when a party [of Bohemians] who had spent the evening at the Cliff House discovered the moon in the act of approaching the earth at a rate that, according to exact astronomical calculations, would have brought that celestial body in sixteen days, eight hours, and thirty-five minutes in contact with the earth. As the clash would take place south of Market Street, and, as that part of the city had already previously suffered from the Second-Street Cut, real estate south of Market Street was falling rapidly.[9]

What little remained of the elegance of Rincon Hill was destroyed in the holocaust of 1906. The quake itself did little damage on the Hill. Even the brick buildings such as the Sailors' Home and St. Mary's Hospital were unharmed. [10] The Rev. F. A. Doane, son of a former sheriff, General Charles Doane, owned a brick residence built in 1860 on the northwest corner of Harrison and Hawthorne Streets: he reported that not only was it undamaged, but even its tall chimneys were not harmed.

For some time, the level district "South of the Slot," between Market Street and Rincon Hill, had been closely built with frame houses and small factories. The large 100-vara lot blocks of that area were mostly cut by small streets, all lined with homes with twenty-five-foot or less frontages. There were few gardens in this densely-packed neighborhood inhabited by the "working class." The area was a tinder box, described in Robert Louis Stevenson's *Cosmopolis* in 1882 as "built of timber . . . a woodyard of unusual extent . . . [where] fires spring up readily." [11]

Immediately after the quake, fires broke out; as there was little or no water available, the fires joined and burned uncontrolled. This fire quickly spread to Rincon Hill, burning everything, including South Park. Destroyed were the homes of a few of the elite who still lingered on, such as Henry Miller's, Jerome Lincoln's, and Irving Scott's. Only on the outskirts of the Hill, a few stone or brick warehouses, such as the Oriental and the Hathaways', survived the fire, as did part of Wieland's Brewery. This latter building, of stone construction behind the Second Street Brewery, remained until the 1960s.

One wooden home still exists, but it is located far away from its original site on Rincon Hill. In the early 1860s, Adolph Weber, a president of the Humboldt Bank and brother of Captain Charles Weber, founder of the city of Stockton, built a home on Folsom Street. In 1891, it was carefully taken down and rebuilt in the Santa Cruz mountains, where it stands today. Preserved by Mrs. Gerald Kennedy, granddaughter of Captain Weber, it remains in her family.

After the disaster of April 1906, Rincon Hill's story is a different tale. Suffice to say, the clamor to level the hill continued, such as the Chamber of Commerce's program in 1922 recommending further cuts. Now the Bay Bridge's western terminal rests on what is left of Rincon Hill, so leveled that it is only a slightly elevated area. As Herb Caen has written, "There's virtually nothing left of Rincon Hill." [12]

NOTES

[1] Rev. Harry Jones ("A London Parson"), *To San Francisco and Back* (London, 1871), pp. 67-68.

[2] B. E. Lloyd, *Lights and Shades in San Francisco* (San Francisco, 1876), p. 107.

[3] John S. Hittell, *A History of the City of San Francisco* (San Francisco, 1878), pp. 379-380.

[4] Gunther Barth, *Instant Cities* (New York, 1975), p. 218.

[5] Malakoff Hill, once over 100 feet high, was located between Second and Third and Brannan and Townsend Streets. It received its name during the Crimean War, as did Malakoff Diggings in Nevada County, now a State Park.

[6] Charles Warren Stoddard, *In the Footprints of the Padres* (San Francisco, 1902), p. 93.

[7] Robert Louis Stevenson, *The Wrecker* (London, 1892), p. 125.

[8] Stoddard, *In the Footprints of the Padres,* pp. 93-94.

[9] H. H. Behr, M.D., *Hoot of the Owl* (San Francisco, 1904), pp. 67-68.

[10] Edward Topham, M.D., *St. Mary's Hospital* (San Francisco, 1950), pp. 21-24.

[11] Robert Louis Stevenson, *San Francisco, A Modern Cosmopolis* (Reprint, San Francisco, 1963), p. 24.

[12] Herb Caen, *Hills of San Francisco* (San Francisco, 1959), p. 6.

Rincon Hill AND South Park

A Photographic Album

Upper left: First Street, 1852. Note that the bay comes up to First Street, hence its name. The building on the right is the Vulcan Foundry, established in 1851 by George Gordon, developer of South Park. The building left center is the Pacific Foundry, founded in 1850 by E.B. Goddard. The bay is filled with ships abandoned by their crews during the Gold Rush.
National Maritime Museum

Lower left: Happy Valley, 1852, showing the prefabricated houses built by Folsom, Brannan and Howard.
Author's Collection

Below: A view of Rincon Hill from Howard Street in 1852. The house standing alone on Second Street near the ridge was that of Henry Halleck, who later became General in Chief of the Union armies during the Civil War. In 1852 the house was occupied by California's first orphanage, the Protestant Orphan Asylum.
Author's Collection

Above: Looking north along Second Street from Folsom on Rincon Hill, 1856. Captain Folsom's home on the left, the newly completed St. Mary's Cathedral (now Old St. Mary's) is the large dark structure in the middle distance. On the far left is the tower of Dr. Willey's Howard Presbyterian Church, one of the first south of Market. Dr. Willey later was a founder of the College of California, now the University of California. *Authors Collection*

Below: Market Street looking south toward Rincon Hill in 1856. On Market Street (right foreground) is St. Patrick's Church, built in 1854, (subsequently moved twice, its present site is Eddy Street) and the substantial brick building next to it is the Roman Catholic Orphanage, both on the site of the present Sheraton Palace Hotel. The white wooden church to the south, behind the orphanage, is Dr. Willey's Howard Presbyterian Church (1850). The white house behind it, standing alone on Second Street, is General Halleck's. On the crest of the Rincon Hill are the dark shapes of mansions belonging to Church, Sather, Selby and Day. *CHS*

Right: After William Ralston bought St. Patrick's Church property on Market Street for his Palace Hotel site, the new St. Patrick's opened on Mission Street near Third Street in 1872. Heavily damaged by the fire of 1906, it was rebuilt, retaining some of the original structure. It still stands, one of the few survivors in the Yerba Buena Redevelopment area. To the far left of the photo is a small building at 762 Mission with a sign that reads: "S.F.L.H. Foundling Asylum." Founded in 1868, the San Francisco Lying-in Hospital and Foundling Asylum cared for "unprotected single women with their offsprings." The trustees were well-known San Franciscans, and on its medical staff were leading physicians including Drs. Beverly Cole, Henry Gibbons, H.H. Toland, and John Morse, Sr. The institution's report of 1878 states that pregnant girls "leave home and come to the city to avoid notice. Upon their arrival they are at once marked as prey of the procuress, procurer and abortionist. The trio named are in league so that if they [the girls] live to leave the abortionist's hands it is only to fall into what is worse than death - prostitution."
Roy Graves Collection

Below: Howard Presbyterian Church on Mission Street. Founded by the Reverend S. H. Willey in 1850 on Natoma Street, it moved to Mission between Third and Fourth Streets in 1867. It soon had the largest Presbyterian congregation in the City. The neighborhood changed and it again moved (in 1896) near Golden Gate Park. The small building to the left is the San Francisco Fruit and Flower Mission (founded in 1880). *CHS*

Above: Dr. Thomas Wade opened the Grand Opera House in 1876 on the north side of Mission, near Third Street. It was quite large, holding 2,500 spectators, and later was enlarged to hold even more. It was at this Grand Opera House on the fateful night of April 17, 1906, that Enrico Caruso was singing. It was the last performance in this theater as it was to be destroyed by the fire. A little alley named "Opera," off Mission near Third Street, is the only physical evidence of the once luxurious theater. *CHS*

Left: On the south side of Howard Street between Second and Third stood the large Howard Street Methodist Church. Organized in 1852, it was first located on Folsom Street. It acquired the Howard Street property in 1862 and built the imposing edifice shown here. To the left, near Second Street, was the Episcopalian Church of the Advent, consecrated in 1861. The first rector was the Reverend F.M. McAllister, a brother of Hall and Cutler McAllister. As they were both wardens, the church was banteringly referred to as the "Church of the Holy McAllisters." *CHS*

Right: Union Hall on Howard Street in 1863. It received its patriotic name during the Civil War, and in this photo a barely visible sign over the portal reads "The Union Shall Be Preserved." In its early years many fashionable affairs were held in its second floor auditorium. During the late 1870s and 1880s, it was the scene of many political meetings of diverse groups such as the Workingman's Party. In its later years it served as Morosco's Variety Theatre. The photo shows the building's other function as well, that of a horsecar depot (complete with stables) for the Mission Dolores and Montgomery Street Line. *CHS*

Below: The north-west corner of Folsom and Second Streets. At 610 Folsom Street, next to the vacant lot, is the home of Captain William C. Talbot, and next to it, part of the home of his partner, A.J. Pope, is visible (614 Folsom Street). They were founders in 1849 of the famous lumber and shipping firm of Pope and Talbot, which still flourishes in the Northwest. On Second Street (at far right) is Captain Folsom's home. The Church of the Advent is behind Talbot's residence, and in the far distance is the Emanu-El Synagogue on Sutter near Powell Street. As it was dedicated in 1866, this picture dates after that time.
Author's Collection

Left: The John Parrott mansion was completed in 1854. Parrott, a banker, was one of the wealthiest men in California at that time. The residence stood at 620 Folsom near Second Street. The family left Folsom Street in 1886.
Courtesy Mrs. Barbara Donohoe Jostes

Above: Next to the Parrott residence was U.S. Senator Milton Latham's mansion at 656 Folsom. Latham had also been a Governor of California. Behind the residence are the back of the Church of the Advent (right) and the back of the Howard Methodist Church on the left. Later this home became the residence of Francis Newlands, U.S. Senator from Nevada, a son-in-law of U.S. Senator William Sharon.
CHS

Left: Seated in the carriage sometime in the early 1880s is Mary Parrott, daughter of John Parrott and wife of the Count Christian de Guigné. The Stauffer Chemical Company was a major holding of the family.
Courtesy Barbara Donohoe Jostes, member of the John Parrott and Joseph Donohoe families of Rincon Hill

Left: The United States Marine Hospital, later The Sailor's Home, on Harrison Street between Main and Beale Streets. The Marine Hospital, when opened in 1853, on Rincon Point, was one of the largest structures in California. Closed after the earthquake of 1868, it became the Sailor's Home in 1876. Undamaged by the earthquake and fire of 1906, it continued in use until 1912. It was demolished in 1919.
Author's Collection

Below: J. Oscar Eldridge and his family moved to this house at 646 Folsom Street after their Second Street home was ruined by the Cut. Mary and Grace Eldridge, shown as young girls in the front yard, became Mrs. Charles Green and Mrs. Sidney Cushing. Eldridge bought this house on Folsom Street from Richard Sneath, an importer, who moved to Fair Oaks (later Atherton) in San Mateo County. The Eldridges moved to San Rafael in the 1880s, and the house became the residence of William T. Sesnon.
CHS

Above: General Sherman made this sketch of his house on Harrison Street. It enabled the author to identify Sherman's home in the photograph below which was in the possession of the California Historical Society. *Author's Collection.*

Below: This home (far right) on Harrison near Fremont Street was built in 1855 by William T. Sherman, the future Civil War general. Sherman at that time was in charge of the Bank of Lucas, Turner, & Co. (The bank building still remains at the north-east corner of Montgomery and Jackson Streets). When the Sherman family left San Francisco in 1857 the home was rented to William Blanding, the father of Gordon Blanding (a son-in-law of Tevis). The house to the right of the Sherman house, hardly visible, was that of Sherman's friend, General Samuel M. Bowman. Bowman left San Francisco during the Civil War, and the house became the residence for ten years of U.S. Senator Eugene Casserly. CHS

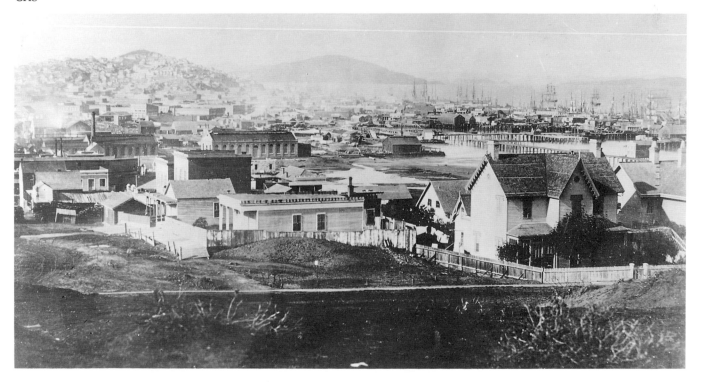

Above: 500 Harrison, the north-west corner of First and Harrison Streets, was the residence of Charles McLane, brother of Louis McLane, and like him general agent of Wells Fargo & Co. Later John W. Farren, a wagon maker and San Francisco supervisor, lived in this mansion. The 500 block of Harrison Street, on the crest of Rincon Hill, became the most fashionable block on the hill.
CHS

Right: The home next to McLane's was the Joseph A. Donohoe mansion, at 526 Harrison Street. Two of his children married into the John Parrott family. The census of 1870 showed Donohoe's household included five servants and a coachman. The Donohoe bank merged into the Bank of America in the 1920s. The house at the far left in the photo was once the residence of historian H.H. Bancroft, and in the 1870s was the home of George Wheaton.
Courtesy Barbara Donohoe Jostes

Above: Library, Joseph A. Donohoe mansion, Harrison Street. Note the portrait of Joseph A. Donohoe I. The painting is now owned by Joseph A. Donohoe IV. It was painted in 1861 by the French artist Jules E. Saintin, who the previous year had painted a portrait of Stephen Douglas.
Courtesy Barbara Donohoe Jostes

Below: Henry Miller, the "Cattle King," built his mansion at the north-west corner of Essex and Harrison Streets in the 1870s. He had the old brick home shown in the previous photo demolished. Miller's mansion was on a grander scale than the older homes on the Rincon Hill, appearing more like the later mansions on Van Ness and Pacific Heights. He was living at this residence on April 18, 1906, and carefully locked the home as the flames approached. His great-grandson, Henry Miller Bowles, inherited the key, the only surviving relic of the home's contents.
Courtesy Henry Miller Bowles

Left: The north-west corner of Harrison and Essex Streets. On the right was the residence of Louis Garnett, father of author Porter Garnett. To the left of it is the Coe-Raymond-Earle home. There were several prominent occupants of this home. One of the earliest was John Tucker, a jeweler and developer of "Tucker Town," a residential enclave that was part of the Western Addition. One of these houses still stands at 2209 Jackson Street. Later in the 1860's, L.W. Coe, a mining speculator, resided here. I.W. Raymond was the next occupant. While Raymond was well-known as a steamship agent, he is best remembered for his efforts to make Yosemite Valley a public park. A mountain peak in Yosemite bears his name. The last occupant before Henry Miller purchased the property and demolished the residence was John O. Earle, who had made a fortune in the Comstock Lode (Gould and Curry and the Ophir mines). As a director and one of the largest stockholders of the Bank of California when Ralston failed, Earle lost much of his wealth. To the left of this residence is the home of General Lucius Allen at 570 Harrison Street. His daughter lived across the street after marrying Jonathan Kittle. 570 Harrison had previously been the residence of Henry Carlton, Jr., an associate of William T. Coleman.
Courtesy Margery Foote Meyer

Below: Edward W. Church's residence at the north-east corner of Second and Harrison Streets was one of the first large homes to be built on Rincon Hill. Church was a partner of Peder Sather in the banking firm of Sather and Church. Church died of typhoid fever in 1861, when he was only 47 years old, but his family continued to reside in the home.
Photograph courtesy of Mrs. Philip Landis, granddaughter of Prentiss Selby and great-granddaughter of Edward W. Church

Above left: The mansion of Irving Scott, general manager of the Union Iron Works, stood at 507 Harrison Street, on the south side. It is said to have been the first home in the City with a private art gallery. The smaller residence to the left was the home of Henry J. Booth, a one time president of the Union Iron Works.
Photograph courtesy of Betty Knight Smith, daughter of Dr. Reginald Knight Smith and granddaughter of Irving Scott

Above: This house was located at 553 Harrison, the south-west corner of Rincon Place. It was the residence of Charles L. Low, brother of Frederick Low, governor of California in 1863-67. Later it was the residence of Peter Donahue's daughter Mamie, the Baroness J.H. von Schroeder. She and her German baron owned the fashionable Hotel Rafael in Marin County for many years.
CHS

Left: This photograph shows the home of Jonathan Kittle at 525 Harrison Street. In 1883 Kittle and his family moved to Ross in Marin County. Their estate in Ross is today the Marin Art and Garden Center. Kittle's daughter Isabel married Benjamin Dibblee, and they also lived in Ross. (Jonathan Kittle's brother was Nicholas Kittle of Second Street on Rincon Hill.)
Courtesy of Isabel Kittle Dibblee

Above left: The residence of Henry S. Dexter at 557 Harrison Street, corner of Stanley Place. Dexter was an engineer for some of the earliest water companies in California. When he left this home it became the residence of Lafayette Maynard, a member of a prominent Southern family in California. Maynard was the grandfather of the famous artist Maynard Dixon. *Author's Collection*

Below left: This imposing Gothic house at 555 Harrison Street was the best remembered by the residents of Rincon Hill whom the author interviewed. In the 1850s it was the residence of Benjamin Horn, brother of Thomas Horn who built a home on Second Street. Thomas Horn's daughter was the noted author Gertrude (Horn) Atherton. In the 1860s this house was the home of William M. Lent, a beneficiary of the Comstock Lode and one of San Francisco's leading capitalists. The last occupants, and the most permanent, were the Jerome Lincolns. They still owned the property in 1906. Lincoln was a long time director of the Bank of California and was also president of Pacific Savings Bank. The photograph shows members of the Lent family in front of the house. *Bancroft*

Below: Captain Millen Griffith's home at 599 Harrison Street from 1859 until his death in 1896. The land was given to the City by the Griffith family for a playground. Try to find it today. *Courtesy Edward (Ted) Griffith*

Above: Banker Peder Sather lived at the north-west corner of Second and Harrison Streets. His home was one of the earliest on Rincon Hill, dating from at least 1854. His residence was damaged by the Cut in 1869. Charles Warren Stoddard wrote, "The ruins I lived in had been a banker's Gothic home" and describes his meetings with Robert Louis Stevenson in 1880 in that "ruin." Sather's second wife made several bequests to the University of California including Sather Gate, the Campanile and the Sather Professorship. His grandsons, who received little from his estate, were not pleased. One, Dr. Peder Sather Bruguiere, told me Mrs. Sather (Jane Krom) was "an adventuress who picked his grandfather up on a ferryboat"! Another landmark house on the crest of Harrison Street was the home of Thomas Selby, one of the first to build a large home on Rincon Hill. Selby founded the Selby Smelting Company, built the Selby Shot Tower and was mayor of San Francisco from 1869 to 1871. A son, Prentiss, married Florence Church, who lived a few houses away. Daughter Clara married A.J. Ralston, brother of William C. Ralston. Selby's home is said to have had the first ball room in San Francisco.
Courtesy Society California Pioneers

Above: Looking west from the 600 block of Harrison Street, showing Rincon Hill to be a real hill. In the distance is smoke from George Gordon's (the creator of South Park) sugar refinery. Located at Harrison and Price (now Eighth) Streets, it was built in 1856, and was the first successful sugar refinery in California. Today near Harrison and Ninth Streets there is a small street named Gordon that recalls the site of this refinery. Twin Peaks is in the distance.
Bancroft

Below left: Residence of Thomas Day at north-east corner of Harrison and Hawthorne Streets. From the 1860s until well into this century the name Thomas Day & Co. was synonymous with fine lighting fixtures. A granddaughter married Anson Blake of Vernon Place. Her father, Frank Symmes, of Day and Co. also resided in this house.
CHS

Below: Peter Donahue's mansion on the north-east corner of Bryant and Second Streets was long the residence of this wealthy family. Donahue had founded Union Iron Works in 1849, the first foundry in San Francisco. Union Iron Works later became Bethlehem Shipbuilding Company and is now owned by Todd Shipyards. With his brother James (of First Street) he founded the first gas works, the forerunner of the Pacific Gas and Electric Company. With Henry Newhall (of Beale Street) he built California's second railroad, the San Francisco - San Jose, completed in 1864. A monument dedicated to this pioneer stands on Market Street. Donahue's second wife, Annie, was a sister of California's seventh governor, John Downey, and of Eleanor Martin, the "Grand Dame" of San Francisco society. With her "Crown Prince" Ned Greenway (of Harrison Street) Eleanor Martin entertained at cotillions that were the social events of the year. Mrs. Martin lived for a time with her sister in the Donahue mansion. The street to the right is Stanley Place (now Sterling). Note the iron deer on the lawn, a sign of affluence in those days. *CHS*

Left: Residence of Louis McLane at 438 Bryant Street. McLane converted two houses into one in 1860, one house being that of Col. Benjamin Washington, collector of the Port of San Francisco. Louis McLane headed Wells Fargo Express for many years and was later president of the Nevada Bank. His father had been Secretary of State and Secretary of the Treasury under President Andrew Jackson. Between 1867 and 1875, when McLane was living in the east, this residence was occupied by the I. Friedlanders, who had moved from South Park. Friedlander was known as the "Grain King." Residing with him was his son-in-law Augustus Bowie, Jr., a mining engineer and the first graduate of St. Ignatius College, now the University of San Francisco.
Author's Collection

Below: In the 1860s this home at 330 Bryant and Rincon Place was owned by Francis Cutting, founder of Cutting Packing Company. Living with him was Sidney M. Smith, who later became owner of the house and president of Cutting Fruit Packing Company. This firm in 1916 became part of the newly formed California Packing Company (Del Monte). Smith's daughter Mrs. Philip Van Horn Lansdale who lived for many years in her mansion at Broadway and Webster gave this photograph to the California Historical Society.
CHS

Above: South Beach in the early 1860s. On the left is St. Mary's Hospital, opened in 1861, and on the right is the U.S. Marine Hospital (Sailor's Home), opened in 1853.
Courtesy St. Mary's Hospital

Below: These two photographs, taken only about ten years later than the photo above from approximately the same place, show the South Beach area completely filled. In the foreground, Malakoff Hill has been leveled except for a small rocky outcrop. In the left background are St. Mary's Hospital on Rincon Hill and the Sailor's Home on Rincon Point. In the center is the Oriental Warehouse and on the right are the Pacific Mail Docks.
Author's Collection

Above: Between 1861 and 1870 South Beach was filled and the Pacific Mail Steamship Docks were built. Near these important wharfs were warehouses. The Oriental Warehouse built in 1868 on Brannan Street survives today. Owners have included the Haslett family, Edgar DePue, and the present owner, his nephew Edgar Osgood. This view from Rincon Hill looking south clearly shows the area.
CHS

Right: The home on the right, at the north-west corner of Second and Brannan Streets, was the home of lumber dealer Samuel D. Blinn. Living in this home with him was his associate William J. Adams. Adams moved a short distance north in the late 1860s. Their holdings included the Puget Sound Packet and the Washington Mill Co. Later, Adam's son met with financial difficulty after his mills burned and his lumber ships were lost. A grandson of William Adams was photographer Ansel Adams. The house on the left, on Brannan Street, was owned by Frank G. Edwards, an importer of carpets and window shades. In 1884 he moved into a lovely house on Guerrero Street, recently beautifully restored. He was a San Francisco Fire Commissioner.
CHS

Below: Homes of Robert F. Rogers and his brother Daniel Rogers on the south side of Brannan between Second and Third Street. Note the hill south of Rincon. This was Malakoff Hill. Robert Rogers was married to a daughter of A.A. Ritchie of South Park. He served in the California Assembly. His brother Daniel was a City Supervisor. They lived here from 1859 to the mid-1870s. Robert Rogers wrote a now scarce book, *My Wife and I;* its contents are such that it is well it is scarce.
Bancroft

Below: St. Rose Academy opened in 1862 on the north side of Brannan Street near Third Street, next to the modest wooden Church of St. Rose. The school moved westward in 1878, the same year the St. Rose Church was rebuilt as an imposing brick edifice. While the church and parish of St. Rose are long gone, St. Rose Academy still flourishes at Pine and Pierce Streets, its location since 1906.
Courtesy Sister Martin Barry, O.P.

Above: Rincon Place ran between Harrison and Bryant Streets. Pictured is the fine house of John Hooper. Other members of the Hooper family also lived on Rincon Hill at various times. Their lumber business was very successful and they later built large homes on Pacific Heights.   *Courtesy Hooper Family*

Below: The residence at 334 Beale Street of Henry Mayo Newhall. Auctioneer, shipping and commission merchant, he founded the Newhall Dynasty. The family is best known because of their vast Newhall Land and Farming Company. The town of Newhall near Los Angeles is named for H.M. Newhall.
Courtesy of a member of the family, Angelica Hill Dunham

Above: Laurel Place (now Lansing Street) was a fashionable street
between First and Essex Streets. Among those living on Laurel Place
were Judge Henry Coon, mayor of San Francisco in 1863–67;
General W.H.L. Barnes, attorney; U.S. Senator Charles Felton, and
Major Richard Hammond, father of the famous John Hays Hammond,
who was born in the Hammond home on Laurel Place.
CHS

Above: Donald C. McRuer lived in this house at 18 Laurel Place. He was associated with the firm of McRuer and Merrill. J.C. Merrill also lived on Rincon Hill, at 14 Stanley Place. McRuer was later president of the California Mutual Marine Insurance Co., and was a City Supervisor, and U.S. Congressman from California in 1864. *CHS*

Above: Residence of Samuel C. Bigelow at
26 Laurel Place, 1858. His daughter the late Mrs.
Samuel Austin Wood stated that the house
windows had been brought "around the Horn"
and that the the first story bays were San
Francisco's earliest bay windows of that type.
Courtesy Helen Wood Pope

Left: A view of the back of 18 Laurel Place (right) in 1883,
when it was the residence of Sarah Althea Hill. This was at the
beginning of her lengthy court case in which she claimed to be
the wife of U.S. Senator William Sharon, banker and owner of the
Palace Hotel. Sharon claimed she was not his wife, but his
mistress. During the trial Sarah married her attorney, Judge David
Terry (who in 1859 had killed Senator Broderick in a duel). The
judge in the case, U.S. Supreme Court Justice Stephen J. Field,
ruled aginst Sarah. Shortly afterwards, the Terrys met Justice Field
at Lathrop, near Stockton and a fight ensued. Terry struck Field
and Field's body guard David Neagle shot Terry, killing him. In
1892, Sarah was confined in the Insane Hospital at Stockton. She
remained there until her death in 1937, forty-five years later. The
city of Morgan Hill is named for her brother. *CHS*

Left: After the Second Street Cut, the Harmon house was moved back from Second Street to Essex Street. The Jennings house is seen on the right. The young lady at the entrance is believed to be Anna Lyle Harmon, later a talented artist.
Courtesy Paul Bearce

Right: Vernon Place (now Dow Street) off Second Street. These homes were built in 1860 by Anson Stiles (Charles Blake's father-in-law) and J. Snowden Bacon. Both lived on Vernon Place. Charles T. Blake (Yale, 1847) came to California in 1849 as a member of George Gordon's Association. After having been an agent for Wells Fargo at Michigan Bluff, he became a successful street contractor in San Francisco. The Blake home was at 4 Vernon Place. Blake's son, Anson Stiles Blake, was not only president of the Society of California Pioneers but also of the California Historical Society. His family built Stiles Hall at the University of California. Anson Blake's estate in Berkeley (Kensington) was given to the University of California and is today the President's home. Another resident of Vernon Place was General James Carleton, commander of the California Volunteer Column during the Civil War.   *CHS*

Below: At 11 Essex, on the corner of Folsom Street, was the William F. Babcock home where Babcock and his family lived from 1853 until the 1880s, when they moved to Marin County. Among his many business activities he was the first president of the Spring Valley Water Company, long the distributor of water to San Francisco. Babcock's family were generous benefactors in Marin County, where their gifts include the William Babcock Memorial Wing of Marin General Hospital.
Courtesy of the late Mrs. Harold McKinnon, granddaughter of William Babcock

Below: Some of the earliest photographs of Rincon Hill show this home with its twin gables and Carpenter Gothic trim. It was located on Essex Place, off Essex Street. Oliver B. Jennings lived here until about 1862, when he returned East. He was a merchant and importer in partnership with Benjamin Brewster. Brewster Jennings, a descendant, gave the California Historical Society a copy of this photograph. The object in the foreground is a pigeon roost. *CHS*

Above: First Street, looking north from Harrison Street in the early 1860s. The church on the ridge line in the far distance is St. Francis Catholic Church, still standing today on Vallejo Street.
Author's Collection

Above: James Donahue residence on 346 First Street. He was co-founder of San Francisco's first gas works and a developer of the Occidental Hotel at Montgomery and Bush Streets, San Francisco's first grand hotel. His grandson Richard Burke aided Richard Dillon in his book *Iron Men*, the history of the Donahue Family.
CHS

Left: Few names in San Francisco are more distinguished than that of McAllister. Hall McAllister, whose statue stands by the City Hall on the street that bears his name, lived at 415 First Street, his brother Cutler, next to him at 417. They had built these homes in 1864 and 1866 and left Rincon Hill in the 1870s. In the 1880s Hall's home was occupied by Captain Richard Floyd (brother of the mother of William Gibbs McAdoo) and his wife Cora who was the daughter of the very wealthy Judge H.A. Lyons, who had given them the home as a wedding present. The Floyds' daughter Harriet created quite a furor in San Francisco society when she married a cable car conductor. Henry George, of "Single Tax" fame, completed his book *Progress and Poverty* in the house at 417 First Street, Cutler's old home, in 1879. A plaque long stood at the site.

This photograph was given to me by Elliott McAllister, 8th president of the Bank of California. It was taken long after the McAllisters had left. A plaque bearing Henry George's likeness marked the site until the San Francisco Bay Bridge was built in the 1930s. It read: Here, in 1878-1879, Henry George "The Prophet of San Francisco" wrote *Progress and Poverty* expounding natural laws that, breached, cause poverty but, obeyed, assure us all peace, progress and plenty. Plaque erected September 8, 1930 by the Henry George Foundation of America.

Below: The Vulcan Foundry, established in 1851 by George Gordon, was long located on First Street. In 1867, when this steam locomotive was built by the Vulcan Foundry, the president was Joseph Moore. He was the founder of the well known family which for many years ran Moore Dry Docks. The locomotive shown, the Calistoga, was built for the Napa Valley R.R. and rebuilt in 1875 as the Vacaville for the Vaca Valley R.R. *Bancroft*

Above left: The Union Iron Works (the first iron foundry in California) was established by Peter Donahue in 1849. This photograph was taken during the years (1866-1873) when Henry J. Booth's name appeared on the building. Booth was associated with the iron works from 1864 when he was living on Vernon Place. Later he lived at 501 Harrison Street. Irving Scott succeeded Booth as the head of this pioneer institution in about 1875. *CHS*

Below: The Selby Shot Tower at First and Mission was long a landmark South of Market. It was erected in 1864 by Thomas Selby, mayor of San Francisco in 1869 and founder of the Selby Smelting Company. The tower stood 200 feet tall and was used in the manufacture of lead shot and bullets. The Miners Foundry was another of the numerous foundries on First Street (Union, Vulcan, Fulton, Pacific and Golden Gate). It was established in 1860 and employed several hundred "hands." *CHS*

Above: In the 1860s this double house on Second Street was occupied by J.O. Eldridge and Bishop William I. Kip. Eldridge was an auctioneer with Newhall and later in real estate (Easton and Eldridge). He also served on the Board of Education, the Park Commission and as a trustee of Mills College. After the Cut destroyed his home, he moved to 646 Folsom Street. The left side of the house was the residence of Bishop Kip. He was Bishop of the Episcopal Church in California for over forty years. After the Cut he moved north of Market Street.

To the north of the double house was the home of the Reverend William A. Scott, who founded both Calvary Presbyterian Church and St. John's Presbyterian Church, both still flourishing in San Francisco. Dr. Scott was not afraid to express his opinion, and as a result was hanged twice in effigy. The first time was in 1856 for criticizing the Second Committee of Vigilance, the second time for expressing his pro-southern sentiments. During the Civil War he left San Francisco and his son-in-law Nicholas Kittle became the occupant of Scott's house. The Kittles moved to Marin County when they were forced out by the Second Street Cut in 1869. The home seen to the right (north) was built by General Henry Halleck at the corner of Folsom. A famous lawyer, he is also known in San Francisco as the builder of the Montgomery Block. During the Civil War Halleck was General in Chief of the Union Army. Later the residence was occupied by Halleck's friend Col. George Grannis of the California National Guard. In 1884, Grannis, an attorney, was administrator of the estate of General Halleck's widow (a grand-daughter of Alexander Hamilton).
Author's Collection

Right: On the left in this lithograph is the home of Captain J.L. Folsom, the largest and finest example of Gothic Revival in the area when it was built in 1852. After Folsom's death in 1856 it became the home of John Wieland. Members of his family continued to live in this home until 1889.   *CHS*

PHILADELPHIA BREWERY.

JOHN WIELAND,
SECOND STREET NEAR FOLSOM, SAN FRANCISCO.

Above: This octagonal house on Second Street near Folsom was one of San Francisco's several octagonal houses, of which only two remain. One is on Russian Hill (Green Street) and the other is at 2645 Gough, near Union Street, and is owned by the Colonial Dames. This one belonged to Cyrus Palmer, a '49er who headed the Pacific Foundry and later the Golden State Foundry. He served as a Supervisor of San Francisco in the 1860s.
Courtesy Dr. John Kemble

Above right: Top of the Hill, i.e. south, of the octagonal house on Second Street was the home of Cyrus' father, William A. Palmer. This house, according to Mrs. A.W. Stetson, daughter of Wales Palmer who was born on Rincon Hill, was brought around the Horn in sections from Portland, Maine, in 1853. Another daughter, Mrs. S.H. Harman, lived in the house on the right. Harman was in the lumber business. The house just south of the Harman's belonged to William Badger, who lived at 333 Second until the Cut. He was a member of the firm of Badger and Lindenberger, importers. Badger served as a school director and was one of the first presidents of the San Francisco YMCA. T.E. Lindenberger also lived at this home in the late 1860s.
Courtesy of Mrs. Stetson and Paul Bearce of Palo Alto

Right: When the news arrived of the assassination of President Lincoln, a parade formed on April 19, 1865. The route was Second Street to Folsom Street, which is shown in this photograph. The marchers then went on Folsom to Third Street, continued on to Union Square. Standing on the Second Street Hill are residents of Rincon Hill; note the silk top hats of the elite and flags at half mast. Old St. Mary's is seen in the background.
Society of California Pioneers

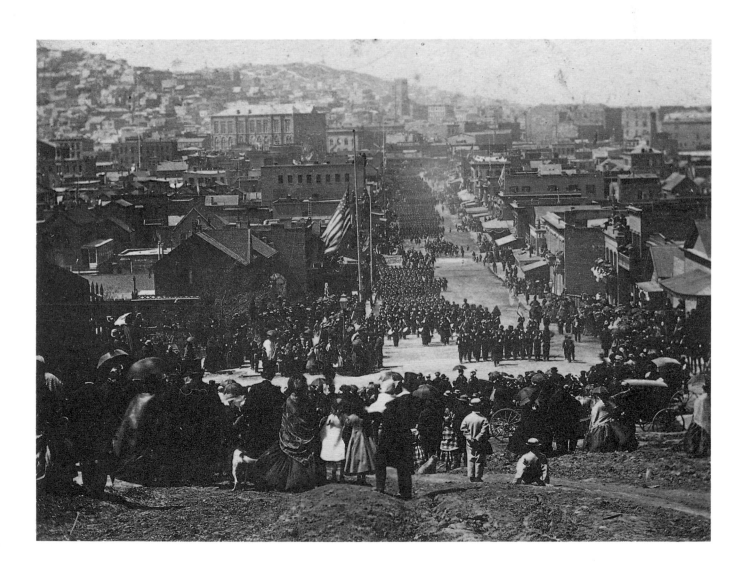

Above left: Residence of Jerome B. Piper, at 15 De Boom Street. Piper was a member of Stevenson's Regiment and arrived in San Francisco in 1847. He served as a San Francisco assistant alderman in 1851 and was president of the Piper Line, bay and river schooners. He also owned a brickyard. He bought this house in 1867 and his family lived there until 1890. His wife and two sons, Frank and Arthur, are in the photograph. The house next door, at 13 De Boom, was owned by George F. Bunker, sea captain. The Bunker family lived there from 1862 to 1886. Naturally the Pipers and Bunkers lived on upper De Boom: the underprivileged lived on lower De Boom, as columnist Herb Caen has written.
Courtesy Harold B. Day, grandson of J.B. Piper

Below left: The Tiger Engine Company on Second Street near Howard was organized in 1855. As a young man, Claus Spreckels, the future Sugar King, was a member of this volunteer fire company.
Author's Collection

Above: Mat Searing was a foreman of the Tiger Company and later a trustee of the Fire Department's Charitable Fund and a director of the Exempt Fire Company in 1866. He poses here with a speaking trumpet, a practical symbol of his authority.
Author's Collection

Left: The Rincon Hose Company, one of San Francisco's many volunteer fire fighting companies, was established in 1864 on Folsom Street near Beale Street. Note the stuffed chicken on top of the hose reel: a mascot, perhaps? In 1866 a paid fire department was created and the colorful volunteer system ceased.
Author's Collection

Second Street, looking south from Market Street, before the infamous Cut was made. Note that the hill was a steep and sizable one, a considerable obstacle for horsedrawn wagons. On the left side of the street is the sign of the office of the well known Dr. James Cogswell. The photo below shows the Second Street Cut 1868, looking north. On the left (with the gable roof) is the home of Frederick Macondray, Jr. He had married a daughter of Faxon Atherton. Across the street are Peder Sather's home and that of Bishop Kip next door. All were ruined by the Cut. *CHS*

Above: Second Street looking south from Market Street, after the Cut, showing the new Harrison Street bridge, which Charles Warren Stoddard called "a bridge still celebrated as a triumph of architectural ungainliness."
Author's Collection

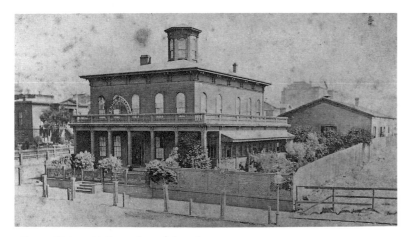

Above: Union College, located at the south-east corner of Second and Bryant Streets. John Middleton, of Second Street Cut ill-fame, lived here in 1861–1862, then leased it in 1863 to the college. The home was then enlarged by the college administrators. Union College, for many years an important school, moved to Berkeley in 1887 where it was merged with Boone's University School.
Author's Collection

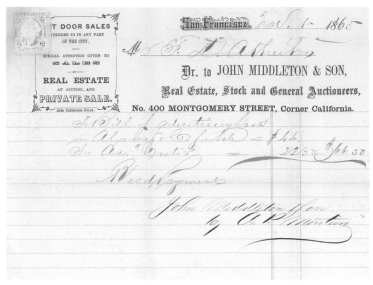

Above: A bill from real estate auctioneer John Middleton to Faxon Atherton for advertising the sale of certain lands in Alameda County in 1865. Middleton, who was elected to the California Assembly in 1867, introduced the legislation that resulted in the Second Street Cut. Faxon Atherton was for a short time a resident of Rincon Hill (Bryant Street) before moving to his country estate located in what is now the town of Atherton.
Author's Collection

Right: Rincon Point Warehouse (also known as Hathaway's) was built in the 1850s and still stands at Spear and Harrison Streets, one of the few surviving buildings of San Francisco's Golden era. It was built by George P. Baker and the Hathaways of South Park, the latter soon becoming the sole owners. It survived in 1875 when a terrible explosion destroyed a nearby building where gun powder was stored. Part of Hathaway's Wharf was destroyed. In 1891 a second story was added to the warehouse.
Author's Collection

RINCON POINT WAREHOUSE,

Office,—No 87 Front Street.

This Warehouse is now ready for the reception and Storage of Grain, Flour, Produce, &c. It is substantially built of brick, and is Fire Proof; having a Wharf front of 275 feet; lying directly in the track of Vessels bound to this City.

Liberal Cash advances will at all times be made, at a low rate of interest, on Grain, Flour, Produce, etc. in store.

Grain, Flour, etc., received direct from the Vessels into the Warehouse, thereby saving the usual expenses of cartage and wharfage.

GEO. T. BAKER.

SAN FRANCISCO, AUG. 6, 1857.

Above: The Silver Street Kindergarten was located on Silver Street (now Stillman Street). Opening in 1878 it was the first free kindergarten in the City. Its first director was Kate Douglas Wiggin, later a noted author whose works include *Rebecca of Sunnybrook Farm*. This institution reflects the changing class structure of Rincon Hill, as it cared for the urchins from what Kate Wiggin called "Tar Flat."
CHS

RINCON HILL

A fashionable neighborhood in the 1860's, Rincon Hill was the home of William Tecumseh Sherman, William C. Ralston, William Gwin, H.H. Bancroft, and others. By the 1880's the Hill, already partially levelled, became a working class district. Today it is nearly invisible beneath the Bay Bridge. This plaque is mounted on the retaining wall of St. Mary's Hospital, built 1861 but destroyed in the fire of 1906.

California Registered Historical Landmark No. 84

Plaque placed by the State Department of Parks and Recreation in cooperation with the Yerba Buena Chapter of E Clampus Vitus and Charles Albert Shumate, April 18, 1981.

Left: This official State plaque was authorized by the State Park Commission on March 29, 1933. The committee approving it consisted of many well known historians including Aubrey Drury, Professor Herbert Bolton, Robert Cowan, Francis Farquhar and Carl Wheat. Not until 1981 was a plaque actually erected on the site of Rincon Hill (on Rincon Place). It was paid for and dedicated with suitable ceremony by the San Francisco Chapter (Yerba Buena #1) of E Clampus Vitus, an organization dating from the California Gold Rush days.
Author's Collection

Above: Rincon Hill, 1906, just before the earthquake and fire. The north side of Harrison Street is shown, including the newly constructed First Finnish Evangelical Lutheran Church (white structure, center left). This ill-fated building was burnt on April 18th, only a few months after it was completed. The new Fairmont Hotel is seen in the distance. Also in the distance is the tower of the Call Building (Spreckels) on Market Street, which still stands in a revised form. The large house with a mansard roof (center foreround) on Harrison Street is the Joseph Donohoe mansion. The Selby Shot Tower on First Street is on the right. The new "skyscraper" in the middle distance on the right is the Mills Building, built in 1892, which still stands on Montgomery Street.
From the New San Francisco Magazine, May, 1906

Below: South of the Slot before the 1906 fire was clearly a district of wooden structures. The 100 vara blocks were cut by small streets, all lined with homes on about twenty-five foot frontages. Robert Louis Stevenson described the area as "built of timber...a woodyard of unusual extent...[where] fires sprang up readily." After the earthquake this district was the first to burn. To the right in the distance was the massive Palace Hotel. To the left of it, on Mission Street, is St. Patricks Church. On the far left is Howard Street. *Author's Collection*

Left: Adolph Weber, brother of Captain Charles Weber, founder of the city of Stockton, was a long time president of the Humboldt Bank in San Francisco. In 1859 he built his residence at 840 Folsom Street. In the early 1890s the house was carefully taken down, moved to the Santa Cruz mountains and rebuilt. It is the sole surviving pre-1906 residence of the Rincon Hill area. It is still owned by descendants of Captain Weber, Mr. and Mrs. Jerry Cole. *Courtesy of the late Mrs. Gerald Kennedy, grand-daughter of Captain Weber*

VIEW OF SOUTH PARK FROM THIRD STREET

Above: An 1854 engraving of South Park, drawn by the Englishman George Henry
Goddard, artist, architect, surveyor and map maker who had designed somewhat similar
additions to the estate of Lord Holland in London.
Author's Collection

Below: This plate of South Park is from John Middleton's "Auction Sale of Real
Estate, October 22, 1860." It shows the incomplete development of that time.
Author's Collection

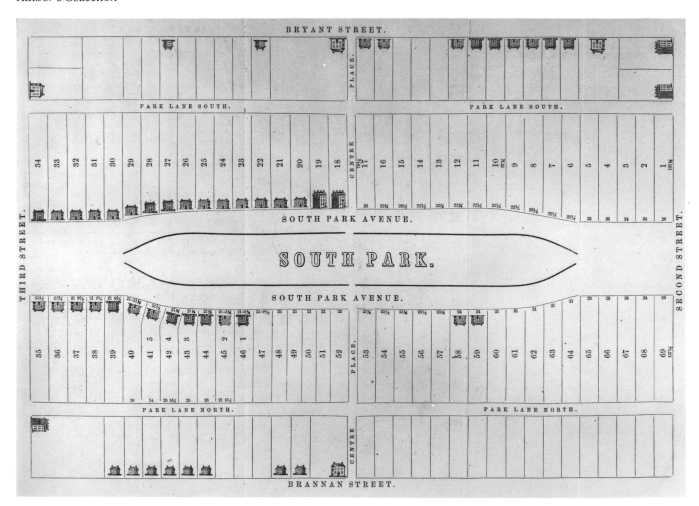

Above: One of the earliest photographs of South Park. The north-west quarter, shown here, was built in 1854 and opened in January 1855. The corner house at Third Street, on the far left, belonged to R.B. Woodward, later famous for his Woodward's Gardens. On the far right the three story structure was the home of Captain Archibald A. Ritchie, owner of vast lands in Solano, Napa and Lake counties. The homes in the distance on the crest of the Hill are those of Thomas Day, Peder Sather and E.W. Church.   *Courtesy of Robert G. Weinstein*

Below: Many Argonauts who came to California during the Gold rush years were from England, France and the Italian Kingdoms, countries allied with Turkey and opposed to Russia in the Crimean War. Thus there was great interest in the war, and when the news finally reached California that Sebastopol had at last fallen in September, 1855, a great celebration was planned. On November 26, 1855, two thousand representatives of the allied countries marched to South Park where a spacious pavilion had been erected. A banquet followed, with wine, beer, and champagne flowing freely. The various nationalities began to fight amongst themselves, resulting in chaos. This early attempt at international goodwill had failed. The engraving of the event is from *The Illustrated London News*, February 16, 1856   *Author's Collection*

Left: George Gordon, whose real name was George Gordon Cummings, led his "California Associates" to California in 1849. In San Francisco he entered the lumber and construction business, and founded the Vulcan Iron Works. He opened South Park in 1855. A year later (1856) he founded California's first successful sugar refinery. The story of the family's decline was the basis of Gertrude Atherton's first novel, *The Randolphs of Redwoods* (1883) later rewritten as *A Daughter of the Vine (1899)*.

Below left: A bill from wood engraver T.C. Boyd to George Gordon for an advertising cut. In 1860 Gordon still had sections of his South Park unsold. In October he offered the seventeen lots between Center and Second Streets, the entire north-eastern quarter. Theodore C. Boyd was an engraver in San Francisco from 1856 to the turn of the century. He was also at times a bookseller and artist. Boyd was long noted as a publisher of broadsides of popular songs, which he often illustrated with humorous figures: among them were The Doony Song; Sally, Come Up; Three Hundred Thousand More; and Grafted into the Army.
Author's Collection

BOYD'S ENGRAVING ESTABLISHMENT.

NOTICE—If an Engraving warps, lay the hollow side of the wood-cut on wet paper, let it remain until it becomes straight. When a wood-cut is PERFECTLY LEVEL, soak it in oil occasionally and it will not warp, as all the pores of the wood will be closed. To clean the cut use Turpentine. T. C. BOYD respectfully informs his customers that he designs and engraves every description of advertising cuts. Views of Buildings, Goods, Wares, Patent Articles, Portraits, Labels, Masonic, Odd Fellow and Temperance Seals, Notary Public and County Seals (brass or wood,) Bill Head, Vignettes, Newspaper Heads, Serious or Humorous Book Illustrations, &c. All fine work done at this establishment is Engraved on Turkey Boxwood imported from New York.

Stamps of all kinds Engraved, Ink Boxes for sale. Orders for Stereotyping attended to.

T. C. BOYD,
Designer and Engraver on Wood.

San Francisco. Oct 12th 1860

Mr George Gordon

To T. C. BOYD, Dr.

To Engraving this cut $10.

Received paymt
T C Boyd

Right: A rare document showing assessment of residents of South Park for watering roads from May to November, 1859. Each of the residents is listed with the dollar amount assessed, followed (in some cases) by the resident's signature. The note at the bottom, signed by George Gordon, reads, "The above work was well and satisfactorily done and at $30 per month less than any other bidder." Residents listed include R.B. Woodward, who built Woodward's Gardens; I. Friedlander, the Grain King; J. R. Redington, wholesale drug merchant; Lloyd Tevis, later president of Wells Fargo; G. Wallace, secretary to Governor Downey; I.C. Davis, cement, later Cowell; James Otis, later mayor of San Francisco; George Johnson, importer and consul to Norway and Sweden, and father-in-law to Kate Johnson, philanthropist; Mrs. Ritchie, widow of Captain A.A. Ritchie, owner of land grants in Solano County and Lake County; David Colton, later of the Southern Pacific Railroad; and of course George Gordon. *Author's Collection*

Below: This photograph, looking east from Third Street, shows South Park at its height, in about 1860. The north-west quarter is completely built and most of the south-west quarter is complete. Gregory Yale, a mining lawyer, lived on the south-west quarter. He wrote the first book on mining laws in the U.S.A. The house on the north-west corner now belonged to importer Alexander Forbes, after Woodward left South Park. *CHS*

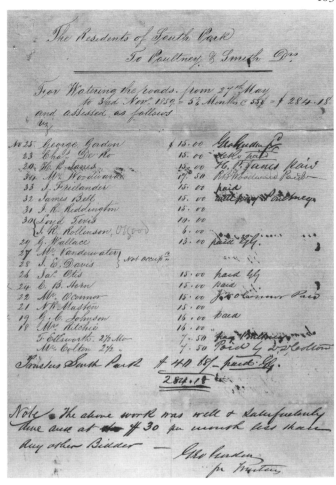

Above: South Park in the 1860s.
California Historical Society

Right: The Miel Institute in South Park. It was opened by the Reverend Charles Miel in 1863. At its opening, a poem by Bret Harte especially written for the occasion was read. Later Miel moved to San Rafael, where he opened a school. Still later he became rector of Christ Church in Sausalito (1891-96). The building in South Park became Mme. Bertha Zeitska's Young Ladies' Seminary in 1867. In 1877 she moved her school north of Market and ten years later returned to her native France. Her school became Miss Lake's School, long a fashionable institution in San Francisco.

Right: This home in the northeast quarter of South Park was made of wood and did not conform to the original plans which called for houses of brick or stone. Celedonio Ortiz lived here in the early 1870s. His daughter married Dario Orena, father of Mrs. James H. Guilfoil. Later in the 1870s the house was the residence of Senator Gwin. In the 1880s and 1890s William M. Smith, a retired sea captain, resided here.
Courtesy Lloyd Brinck, grandson of Captain William Smith and Irene Neasham

Below: South Park in 1889, showing the south side from Second Street, looking west. Miels' old institute is shown and further west a new wooden building with flats has been erected.
Author's Collection

Above: South Park in the 1890s The iron fence
around the park has disappeared. Wooden houses,
some with flats, have been built.
Author's Collection

Below: South Park shortly before the 1906 fire. Flats have replaced the homes
and eucalyptus trees have replaced the former planting. South Park was now a
working man's district, although still a pleasant residential neighborhood.
From the 31st Annual Report of the Board of Park Commissioners 1902, P32

Above: South Park after the 1906 fire. Note the almost total destruction. The wooden houses burned completely and only crumbling shells of some of the brick structures remain. Tents have been erected in the park for the military.
Author's Collection

Below: Wooden buildings replaced the tents in South Park shortly after the disaster. Nineteen wooden buildings opened on November 15, 1906, containing 656 rooms. By March, 1907, they were housing 648 refugees.
Author's Collection

Above: Statement from Mme. Herrera to Faxon Atherton. The South Park Young Ladies' Seminary of Madame Maria Herrera was located at Bryant and Second Street. It was established at least from 1859, and continued until 1865. However she had a school on Dupont (Grant) in 1854. Her husband Francisco Herrera was editor of a Spanish newspaper, a book dealer, and consul of Colombia, Nicaragua, Bolivia and Costa Rica at various times. He was also a teacher of Spanish. Isabel, the daughter of Faxon Atherton married Enrique Edwards of Chile. She was seven years old when she attended Madame Herrera's school.

Author's Collection

Below: Statement from the South Park Livery Stable. George Poultney's livery stables were the best known in the South Park vicinity. They were located on Brannan Street, between Second and Third Streets in the 1850s. Later in the 1860s, while on Bryant Street, they were known as Tattersall's Livery Stable. In the later years they were opposite South Park at 524 Third. This bill is made out to George Gordon who created South Park.

Author's Collection

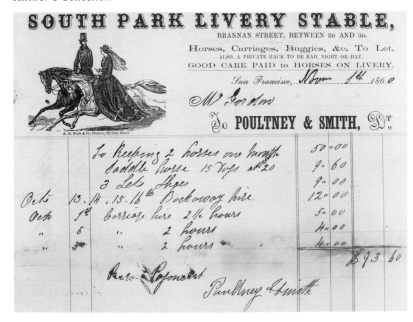

Some of the prominent early day residents of Rincon Hill and South Park. Names indicate heads of households and in most cases include families. Business and professional affiliations of those listed are indicated; specific positions or offices held are noted only when they are a matter of record. Fragmentary biographical notations sometimes included here testify to the diversity and vigor of life as men and women lived it during the glory days of Rincon Hill and South Park.

Adams, William J.
2nd Street near
Brannan Street 1861-68
Lumber (Grandfather of
photographer Ansel Adams)

Adler, Morris
N.E. corner Folsom &
Beale Streets 1859-70s
Rincon Market

Alexander, General Barton S.
30 South Park 1867-77
U.S. Army

Allen, General Lucius
618 Harrison Street 1862-70s
570 Harrison Street 1870's-90s
Daughter: Mrs. Jonathan Kittle
Granddaughter: Mrs. Benj. Dibblee.

Almy, Andrew J.
South Park 1856
643 Folsom Street 1859-62
Redington & Co.

Alvord, William
564 Folsom Street 1859-83
Pres., Bank of California,
Mayor of San Francisco

Applegarth, William
47 South Park 1870-72
Mining

Arrington, William
643 Folsom Street 1875-79
252 2nd Street 1880
Wells, Fargo & Co.

Ashbury, Monroe
S.W. corner Folsom &
Essex Streets 1856-60
City Supervisor
Ashbury Street namesake

Ashe, Dr. Richard P.
44 South Park 1862-65
540 2nd Street 1870s
Physician (His wife was sister
of Admiral David G. Farragut.
Children included Porter,
Gaston & Mrs. Norman McLaren)

Aspinall, Benjamin
S.E. corner Folsom &
Essex Streets 1856-61
Shipping

Atherton, Faxon Dean
N.E. corner 2nd &
Bryant Streets 1860-61
(Peter Donahue's home)

Atwood, George A.
224 2nd Street &
213 Fremont Street 1860s
Engineer

Avery, Harris J.
430-436 Fremont Street 1856-66
Stoves & Tinware

Babcock, William F.
11 Essex 1852-86
Pacific Mail SS Co. &
Pres., Spring Valley Water Co.

Bacon, Jacob Snowden
Commission Merchant; Yale 1847,
(died 1865, family continued
to live at same address)

Badger, William G.
333 2nd Street 1855-70
Badger & Lindenbergen, Importers

Bancroft, Hubert H.
530 Harrison Street 1859-62
Historian, Publisher

Barkeloo, John
South Park 1859-61
Real Estate

Barnard, Thomas G.
23 Hawthorne Street 1856-69,
32 Rincon Place 1870-83
Contractor

Barnes, General William H.L.
403 Bryant Street 1863-65,
20 & 30 Laurel Place 1866-71
Attorney

Batchelder, Joseph M.
Fremont Street, near
Folsom Street 1860
Lumber

Bateman Isaac
555 Harrison Street 1874-79
Stockbroker

Baugh, Washington & Theodore
25 South Park 1865-69
Merchant Exchange

Beck, David
18 Stanley Place 1862-88
Importer

Bell, James
32 South Park 1856-62
Importer with Falkner & Bell,
later Balfour & Guthrie

Benham, Calhoun
420 1st Street 1874-76
Attorney

Bennett, R.H.
Essex Place 1859-67
Commission Merchant

Berton, Francis
11 South Park 1874-77
Banker & Swiss Consul
His daughter was
Baroness de Montchoisy

Bichard, Nicholas
N.E. Corner 1st &
Harrison Streets 1864-90
Shipping, Coal and Lumber

Bierce, Ambrose
775 Harrison Street 1877
Writer

Bigelow, Samuel C.
26 Laurel Place 1859-65
Real Estate, Lumber

Bishop, Thomas B.
236 2nd Street 1870,
536 2nd Street 1871-78
Attorney

Bissell, George
N. Side Folsom St., between
2nd and 3rd Streets 1859-61
Commission Merchant

Blake, Anson Stiles
4 Vernon Place 1870-81
Contractor

Blake, Charles T.
4 Vernon Place 1860-80
Street Contractor
49er & father of Anson Blake

Blake, William P.
Union College, 2nd &
Bryant Streets 1864-65
Professor of Mining

Blanding, William
Rented Gen. Sherman's home,
410 Harrison Street, late 1850s
Attorney
Father of Gordon Blanding,
who married a Tevis

Blinn, Samuel P., & later his widow
542 2nd Street 1863-83
Lumber, partner of William Adams

Boole, George
Various addresses on
Rincon Hill 1860's-70s
Ship Builder

Booth, Henry J.
1 Vernon Place 1864-65,
501 Harrison Street 1866-76
President, Union Iron Works

Bourn, William
Fremont near Folsom Streets 1859,
537 3rd Street near
Brannan Street 1860-70
Merchant

Bourne, Elisha W.
428 Bryant Street 1860-1876
Merchants Mutual Insurance

Bowie, Augustus T., Jr.
438 Bryant Street 1869-75
Mining Engineer

Bowman, Arthur
26 Essex Street 1867-73
Real Estate

Bowman, Charles C.
9 Vassar Street 1863-65
Mining

Bowman, E.P.
9 Vassar Street 1860-66
Broker

Bowman, James
21 Silver Street 1862-65
Attorney

Bowman, General Samuel M.
410 Harrison Street 1856-59
Attorney, Civil War General

Boyce, Thomas
526 Bryant Street 1859-89
San Francisco Supervisor

Brandon, Joseph R.
S.W. Corner Folsom and
Hawthorne Streets 1859-61
Attorney

Brannan, Mrs. A.L.
610 Folsom Street 1873-87

Brannan, Sam
2nd Street, between Minna and
Natoma Streets 1859-60
Entrepreneur

Brewster, R.E.
Essex Place 1855-60
Brewster and Jennings

Brooks, Benjamin
631 Harrison Street 1861-85
Attorney

Brooks, Henry B.
661 Howard Street 1862-64,
776 Folsom Street 1865-72
Odd Fellows' Bank

Bromley, George T.
330 Brannan Street 1871-74
Contractor, U.S. Consul to China

Brown, W.E.
739 Harrison Street 1867-69
Governor Stanford's Secretary

Brumagim, Mark
Tehama Street between 1st &
2nd Streets 1859
Banker

Bryan, William T.
606 Folsom Street 1886-89
Superintendent, Oriental &
Occidental Steamship Company

Bugbee, Samuel C.
14, then 20 Hawthorne
Street 1864-73
Architect

Bunker, George B.
13 De Boom Street 1862-1886
Sea Captain

Burgess, Oscar O., MD
214 1st Street 1868-69,
523 Folsom Street 1870
President, California State
Medical Society

Burnett, Robert
424 Beale Street 1861-62
Alsop & Company

Cabrera, Eduardo
44 South Park 1877-78
Importer

Callahan, Mathias
760 Folsom Street 1860-62
Importer

Campbell, John
312 Brannan Street 1863-78
Pope & Talbot Lumber

Card, Stephen
38 South Park 1860-62
President, Tugboat Company

Carlton, Henry, Jr.
570 Harrison 1856-70
Coleman & Company

Carlton, General James H.
2 Vernon Place 1864-65
Civil War Commander of the
California Column, U.S. Army

Carrigan, Andrew
845 Mission Street 1860-64
Hardware Merchant;
Dunham, Carrigan & Hayden

Casserly, Eugene
410 Harrison Street 1861-70
Attorney, U.S. Senator

Cheesman, David
23 Hawthorn 1860-68
Treasurer, San Francisco Mint

Cheesman, Morton
17 Stanley Place 1864-74,
324 Fremont Street 1878
Banking and Real Estate

Cheever, Henry A.
26 Essex near
Harrison Street 1856-74
Ship Broker, Mining
(Family lived there through 1892)

Choynski, Isidor N.
44 3rd Street and
524 Howard Street 1870s
Antiquarian Bookstore

Church, Edward
N.E. corner 2nd &
Harrison Street 1856-67
Banker, Sather & Church
(Family lived there until 1868)

Church, Seymour (son of Edward
572 Harrison Street 1876-80
Coal Dealer

Coe, L.W.
Harrison and Esex Streets 1865
Imperial Mine (Virginia City)

Coffee, Andrew
17 South Park 1882-85,
640 Folsom Street 1886-89
Notary Public

Cole, R. Beverly, MD
58 South Park 1857-58
President, American
Medical Association

Coleman, Evans
507 Harrison Street 1873,
7 South Park 1874-77,
618 Harrison Street 1878-79
Banker, (Gwin's son-in-law)

Coolidge, Joseph
28 Laurel Place 1860-61,
420 2nd Street 1864-65
Lumber

Coon, Henry
Laurel Place 1860,
620 Harrison Street 1864
9th Mayor of San Francisco

Cooper, Samuel E., MD
660 Mission Street 1859-62
Cooper Medical School

Colton, David
South Park 1860-62,
220 3rd Street 1862-67
Attorney, Southern Pacific R R

Cornwall, Pierre B.
Rincon Place & Harrison St. 1860,
609 Harrison Street 1869-90
Stockbroker; Regent Univ. of Calif.

Crooks, Mathew
Crooks off Townsend, between
3rd & 4th 1859-76
South Park 1876-79
Real Estate

Crowell, Eugene
313 2nd Street 1863-65
Langley & Company (Drugs),
San Francisco Supervisor

Curry, John
528 Bryant Street 1867-68,
450 Bryant Street 1870-86
Sporting Goods

Cutting, Francis
330 Bryant Street 1861-78
President, Cutting Packing Co.

Cutting, Lewis
332 Bryant Street 1861-90
Cutting Packing Co.

Czapkay, Louis
664 Mission Street 1859-64
Medical Institute

Dall, Captain William L.
Various addresses,
Rincon Hill 1859-65
Sea Captain

Dana, William A.
26 South Park 1864-65,
33 South Park 1866-68
Commission Merchant

Davis, George
27 South Park 1868-69
Golden Gate Flour Mill

Davis, Horace
27 South Park 1860-67
Banker, U.S. Congressman

Davis, Isaac
28 South Park 1857-86
Lime and Cement,
later Cowell Cement

Day, Thomas
628 Harrison Street
(N.E. corner of
Hawthorne Street) 1861-71
(Family lived there until 1876)
Lighting Fixtures

De Boom, Cornelius
2nd and South Park 1856
Belgian Consul General,
Real Estate

Decker, Peter
47 South Park 1867-74,
417 1st Street 1876-77
Banker

Dexter, Henry S.
557 Harrison St. 1860s to 70s
S.F. Water Company

Dickie, George W.
674 Harrison Street 1873,
610 Harrison Street 1875
Shipbuilder

Doane, General Charles
42 Hawthorne, N.W. Corner
of Harrison Street
Sheriff of San Francisco
(Family owned house until 1906)

Donahue, James
346 1st Street 1860-62
President, First
San Francisco Gas Works

Donahue, Peter
454 Bryant Street 1860-89
President, Union Iron Works

Donohoe, Joseph A.
N. side Folsom between
2nd & 3rd Streets 1860-61,
526 Harrison Street 1862-95
Banker

Dow, William H.
W. Side of 2nd Street, between
Harrison & Folsom St. 1852-60
Merchant

Doyle, John
430 Bryant Street 1859-63
Retired Teacher

Doyle, John T.
430 Bryant Street 1864-70
Attorney

Drinkhouse, J.A.
409 Bryant Street 1861,
42 South Park 1862-90
Wholesale Tobacco and Cigars

Duperu, Numa
28 Rincon Place 1866-75,
508 2nd Street 1875-82,
28 Stanley Place 1883-85
Stockbroker

Dupouey, Hyppolite, Jules
and Henri
336 2nd Street 1861-62
Union College

Durbrow, Joseph, Jr. & Henry
Essex near Folsom Street 1859-62
Parrott & Company
Grandson, Ambassador Elbridge
Durbrow

Dwinelle, John W.
438 2nd Street 1875-84
Attorney, Judge, Mayor of Oakland

Earl, John Ogden
34 Essex 1870-76
Mining speculator
(Largest stockholder in Bank
of California when it failed)

Eastman, Cyrus A.
28 Hawthorne 1859-79
Mining, later Architect

Eaton, Cornelius J.
330 Fremont Street 1856-76
Mining
(Grandaughter: Mrs.Upton Sinclair)

Eaton, Frederick W.
27 Essex Street 1862-70
Insurance

Eaton, I. Ward
24 Essex Street 1856-67
Real Estate

Eaton, Noble (son of I. Ward Eaton)
24 Essex Street until 1872
Bank of California

Edwards, Frank G.
3008 Brannen Street 1868-84
Carpet Importer

Eells, Rufus
331 Fremont 1856-61
22 Stanley Place 1862
Importer

Eldridge, J. Oscar
44 Minna Street 1859-65
336 2nd Street 1866-69
646 Folsom Street 1870-78
Real Estate Auctioneer

Ellery, Epes
736 Folsom Street 1860-69
Antiquarian Book Store

Ellis, Moses
642 Folsom Street 1859-62
Importer

Emanuel, Lewis
48 South Park 1866-75
Bedstead Factory

Esberg, Mendel
627 Folsom Street 1868-69
645 Folsom Street 1869-75
Tobacco Importer

Estill, General James M.
3rd & Tehama Streets
(family until 1860)
State Senator

Ewing, Charles
445 Bryant Street 1867-70
29 Silver Street 1874-85
Optical Goods

Ewing, John
445 Bryant Street 1871-77
Fire Arms Dealer

Fair, Laura
Laurel Place 1866-67
(Murdered A.P. Crittenden, 1870)

Farnham, John N.
409 1st Street 1868-77
Shipwright

Farnsworth, S. Seymour
20 Laurel Place 1868-83
Sea Captain

Farren, John W.
316 1st Street 1867-85
500 Harrison Street 1886-90
Wagon Maker, later Banker &
San Francisco Supervisor

Faulkner, Evelyn R.
33 South Park 1861-62
Commission Merchant

Felton, Charles N.
413 2nd Street 1868-69
26 Laurel Place 1870
U.S. Senator

Feuerstein, Rudolph
Hawthorne Street near
Folsom Street 1860-62
Sugar Importer

Flint, Edward P.
526 Harrison Street 1856-61
Flint, Peabody & Company,
Commission Merchants

Flint, E.T.
526 Harrison Street 1861
Commission Merchant

Flint, William K.
E. side of Essex St. 1859-60
Commission Merchant

Fisher, Lamer W.
40 South Park 1861-64
Banking, Stockbroker

Fisher, William H.
16 South Park 1875-78
Pacific Transfer Company

Floyd, Captain Richard S.
415 1st Street 1873-89
Capitalist; married Judge
H.A. Lyons'daughter Cora

Folsom, Captain J.L.
2nd St. near Folsom, 1852-55
Landowner; town of
Folsom bears his name

Forbes, Alexander
N.E. corner South Park &
3rd Street 1860-74
Importer

Forbes, Andrew
14 Essex Street 1856-82
Agent, Pacific Mail
Steamship Company

French, Joseph M.
25 Hawthorne St. 1864-68
649 Folsom 1869-71
Importer

Friedlander, Isaac
30 South Park 1858-1867
438 Bryant Street 1867-75
Grain King

Fuller, William Parmer
335 Beale Street 1862-68
322 Beale Street 1868-74
613 Folsom Street 1877-84
Paints, Glass

Gallagher, John
439 1st Street 1873-90
Cooper

Gallagher, Thomas
21 Rincon Place 1875-89
Capitalist

Garnett, Louis
35 Essex Street 1860-97
President, refinery works
(father of author Porter Garnett)

Garrison, William R.
3rd Street at Tehama Street 1859-6
Banking, Shipping,
Mayor of San Francisco

Gawley, William H.
417 Harrison Street 1859-79
Lumber

Gaxiola, Nicholas
20 South Park 1870-95
Consul to El Salvador,
Commission Merchant

George, Henry
625 Harrison Street 1876-77
417 2nd Street 1879-80
Author, Economist

Gibbons, Henry, M.D.
730 Howard Street 1864-1868
Medical Editor &
Professor of Medicine

Gibbs, George W.
400 Harrison Street 1866-71
Consul to Turkey, Importer

Gilmore, George
547 Howard Street 1862-70
Box Factory

Goodsell, De Coury
429 1st Street 1856-93
Real Estate

Gordon, George
20 South Park 1856-59
25 South Park 1860-61
35 South Park 1862-63
Sugar Refiner

Gordon, James E.
27 South Park 1871-72
318 First Street 1872-78
Importer, Hardware

Gordon, Joseph
638 Folsom Street 1866-68
Banker

Grant, Adam
(father of Joseph Grant)
410 Harrison Street 1870
Capitalist

Grant, Charles
322 Fremont Street 1856-76
Empire Granite Works

Granniss, Col. George W.
326 2nd Street 1871-75
19 Hawthorne Street 1875-90
Attorney

Gray, Rev. John
27 Stanley Place 1887
616 Folsom Street 1889
Rector, Church of the Advent

Greenway, Edwin M. (Ned)
665 Harrison Street 1878-79
Wine Distributor, Socialite

Griffin, D.F.
605 Harrison Street 1864-65
Empire Mill & Mining

Griffith, Millen
569 Harrison Street 1859-96
Shipping

Guerin, Michael
459 Bryant Street 1859-78
Importer, Boots & Shoes

Gunnison, Andrew J.
421 Harrison Street 1863-73
Attorney

Gwin, Senator Wm. M.
507 Harrison Street 1869-73
618 Harrison Street 1878-79
7 South Park 1874-76
U.S. Senator

Harnden, Sarah
23 Natoma Street 1856-59
Widow of W.F. Harnden, married
Judge S.C. Hastings

Hager, John S.
501 Harrison Street 1877-78
U.S. Senator

Hahn, Eugene
17 South Park 1885-89
Newspaper Reporter

Haight, Henry
24 South Park 1861
139 Silver Street 1862
Banker & Notary Public

Hale, Henry M.
Bryant & 2nd Streets 1859
Commission Merchant, Bond & Hale

Hall, Isaac
424 Bryant Street 1859-66
Produce, Fruit

Halleck, General Henry
326 2nd Street 1851-69
Attorney & Union Army General

Hallidie, Andrew G.
774 Howard Street 1863-64
Wire Works, Inventor of Cable Car

Hamilton, Miss Alice
Hamilton, Miss Maggie
(became Lady Waterlow, wife
of the Lord Mayor of London)
416 Harrison Street 1877-82

Hammond, Major Richard P.
Laurel Place 1865-67
(father of John Hays Hammond,
who was born on Laurel Place.
Wife was sister of Col. Jack Hays,
first sheriff of San Francisco)
Assemblyman, later with
Southern Pacific RR

Hammond, William H., M.D.
859 Mission Street 1862-87
Physician

Hanlon, Dan
11 South Park 1879-86
Mining

Haraszthy, Agoston
N. side Harrison Street,
between 2nd & 3rd Streets 1856
Father of California Viniculture

Hare, Charles
505 Harrison Street 1863-84
Anchors & Chains
Family lived at this address
until 1890s

Harmon, A.K.P.
423 Harrison Street 1870-73
Mining

Harmon, Samuel H.
331 2nd Street 1859-69
3 Essex Place 1870-95
Lumber
Married Mary Palmer of 2nd St.

Harpending, Asbury
324 Fremont Street
(Ralston's Home) 1870-73
Participant in "Great Diamond Hoax"

Harrison, William P.
35 South Park 1869-70
Wholesale grocer

Harte, Bret
315 2nd Street 1861
Author

Haskell, Edward W.
416 2nd Street 1870-81
Real Estate, Mining

Hathaway, Charles W.
33 South Park 1863-71
Hathaway Wharf & Warehouse

Hathaway, Edward V.
308 Beale Street 1860-62
39 South Park 1863-66

Hathaway, Edmund
308 Beale Street 1863-65

Hawley, Charles A.
313 2nd Street 1856-69
Hardware

Hawley, Charles J.
567 Mission Street 1860s
Groceries

Hawley, David M.
Park Place, off 2nd St. 1856
2nd Street & Folsom 1859-64
Hardware

Hawley, Edward
41 South Park 1862-64
32 South Park 1865-76
Hardware

Hawley, George
32 South Park 1864-76
Hardware

Hawley, Walter
960 Howard Street 1868-75
Hardware

Heath, Richard W.
South Park 1856-57
Tobacco Importer,
Consul: El Salvador & Costa Rica

Herrera, Francisco W.
446 Bryant Street 1856-67
542 Howard Street 1868-75
Consul to Columbia, Editor

Heyer, Albert
10 Silver Street 1864-65
501 Bryant Street 1867-92
Grocer

Hill, Sarah Althea
18 Laurel Place 1883
Senator Sharon's "friend"

Hinckley, Daniel
518 Folsom Street 1861
528 Howard Street 1866
Fulton Iron Works

Hirschfeld, William
627 Folsom Street 1867-73
Jeweler

Hitchcock, Charles E.
9 Laurel Place 1861-70
Importer, Consul Sandwich Islands

Hitchcock, Dr. Charles M.
South side Harrison Street
near 3rd 1860
Physician;
father of Lillie Hitchcock Coit

Hittell, Theodore H.
726 Folsom Street 1860-77
Attorney & Historian

Hochkofler, Rudolph
30 Hawthorne Street 1860-70
Attorney, Consul to Chili,
later to Austria

Hoelsher, August
230 2nd Street 1859-69
Wieland's Beer

Holdredge, William
565 Folsom Street 1863-65
President, Fireman's Fund Ins.
later President, Home Insurance

Holladay, Jessie
316 Fremont Street 1863-65
346 Beale Street 1869
Associated with brother Ben,
the Stage Coach King

Holladay, Samuel W.
416 Bryant Street 1859-61
Hawthorne St. near Folsom 1859
City Attorney
Hooker, Charles G.
523 Folsom Street 1864-67
Importer

Hooker, Richard C.
47 South Park 1876-1880
Stockbroker

Hooper, Arthur
512 Folsom 1871-77
557 Harrison 1878-87
Wholesale Grocery

Hooper, Charles A.
512 Folsom 1866-68
20 Rincon Place 1870-76
557 Harrison 1877-78
Lumber

Hooper, F.P.
512 Folsom Street 1864-68
557 Harrison Street 1878-87
Lumber

Hooper, George & George W.
413 2nd Street 1866-70
512 Folsom Street 1864-66
20 Rincon Place 1871-83
557 Harrison Street 1883-89
Lumber

Hooper, John A.
30 Rincon Place 1861-71
520 Howard Street 1863
512 Folsom Street 1864-66
20 Rincon Place 1870-88
Lumber, Warehouse

Hooper, John
557 Harrison Street 1878
Lumber; (he had six sons)

Hooper, Joseph
413 Second Street

Hooper, William H.
30 Rincon Place 1866
512 Folsom 1867-69
Lumber

Hopkins, Casper T.
30 Rincon Place 1861-65
President, California
Insurance Company

Horn, Benjamin C.
South Park 1858
555 Harrison Street 1859-67
Importer, Cigars

Horn, Thomas L.
East side 2nd near
Harrison Street 1859-60
Importer, Tobacco
Brother of Benjamin Horn,
father of Gertrude Atherton

Houston, A.H.
20 Rincon 1859-69
Construction;
San Jose - S.F. Railroad

Howard, George
Happy Valley 1849-early 50s
Commission Merchant

Howard, William D.M.
Happy Valley 1849-early 50s
Commission Merchant

Howell, Edward S.
25 Hawthone Street 1860-62
Importer

Howell, Mathias
427 Bryant Street 1863-65
Grandfather of George Cabanis

Howland, William H.
319 1st Street 1862-70
Miner's Foundry

Huddart, Dr. R. Townsend
501 2nd Street 1863-75
Union College

Hutton, J.F.
1st & Harrison Street 1852-54
Commission Merchant

Janes, Horace P.
20 South Park 1859-62
Attorney
Mrs. H.P. Janes (widow)
424 Bryant Street 1863-65

Jenkins, Mrs. A.M.
27 South Park 1878-79

Jenkins, James
Folsom Street
between 1st & 2nd St. 1854-56
Mining

Jennings,Oliver B.
Essex Place,
off Essex Street 1853-62
Merchant

Jewett, W.C.
Townsend Street
between 2nd & 3rd 1855
Notary Public

Jewett, Wiliam S.
Corner of Fremont &
Harrison Streets 1856
Artist

Jones, Michael P.
626 Harrison Street 1862-70
418 Fremont Street 1872-80
Wholesale Grocer

Jones, Simon L.
570 Harrison Street 1870-73
Commission Merchant

Johnson, George
19 South Park 1859-72
Importer, Iron & Steel
Consul to Norway & Sweden

Johnson, Robert C. (Son of George)
19 South Park 1873-1875
Importer
Married Kate Birdsell

Johnston, General Albert Sidney
30 Rincon Place 1860-61
General, Union Army & Later of
Confederate Army

Johnston, William B.
11 Essex Street 1856-65
14 Stanley Place 1865
336 2nd Street 2868-69
19 Hawthorne Street 1871-80
Insurance

Jordon, Rudolph
East side 2nd street
at De Boom 1859-64
Tobacco

Josselyn, George M.
512 Folsom Street 1856-65
Ship Chandler

Keeney, Charles C., M.D.
and son, James E. Keeney MD
562 Folsom Street 1860-83
(Brother-in-law of Mayor
William Alvord)

Keene, James R.
12 Essex Street 1868-71
Stock Speculator

Kellogg, Charles W.
4 Essex Street 1859-62
with Wells, Fargo & Co.

Kellogg, George H.
Essex 1856-62
Flint, Peabody & Company

Keller, Levi
231 lst street 1860-68
Commission Merchant

Kentfield, Edwin, George, & John
333 Fremont Street 1859-1906
Shipping

Kerr, Thomas
366 Brannan Street 1862-65
Sugar

Kimball, Thomas N.
415 Harrison Street 1867-77
Mining

Kimball, Thomas L.
314 Fremont Street 1871-76
Mining

Kimball, Solomon
529 Fremont Street 1861-77
Metallurgical Works

King, James C.
40 South Park 1864-66
547 Folsom Street 1867
Shipping

Kip, Rt. Rev. William Ingraham
338 2nd Street 1859-69
Episcopal Bishop of California

Kittle, Jonathan G.
525 Harrison Street 1876-85
Phoenix Iron Works

Kittle, Nicholas
332 2nd Street 1864-69
Shipping & Commission Merchant
Son-in-law of Rev. Wm. A. Scott

Klinkofstrom, Martin
29 South Park 1863-77
Russian Consul

Knight, Samuel & later his widow
435 Bryant street 1861-72
Express Company, San Francisco
(Killed in explosion at Wells, Fargo)

Knowles, Dr. C.C.
25 Silver Street 1859-68
Dentist

Kohn, Isaac
616 Folsom Street 1860-87
Merchant

Korbel (brothers)
437 Brannan Street 1867-76
Cigar Boxes & later Wine Merchants

Kostromitinoff, Peter S.
18 Essex Place 1859-1863
Russian Consul

Ladd, W. Frank
22 South Park 1862-77
Stockbroker & Commission Merchant

Ladd, Wilbur
S.W. corner 1st &
Folsom Streets 1863-66
Real Estate

Lane, Dr. Levi
656 Mission Street 1861-80
Founder Cooper Medical School
(now Stanford Medical)

Langley, Charles
East side Fremont Street,
near Folsom Street 1859-60
662 Harrison Street 1861
Langley & Michael (Drugs)

Lammond, Miss Margaret
353 3rd Street 1862
231 2nd Street 1863-66
Principal, California
Collegiate Institute,
Silver Street, S. F.

Latham, Senator Milton
656 Folsom Street 1864-78
U.S. Senator

Lathrop, Reverend H.D.
426 2nd Street 1878-79
Church of the Advent, Howard St.

Lawton, Theodore
643 Folsom Street 1859-70
With a Commission Merchant Firm

Lent, William H.
24 South Park 1856-59
555 Harrison Street 1868-71
Capitalist

Leonard, Joseph B.
E. side Hawthorne Street 1859-60
Superintendent, Industrial School

Levy, Walter H.
661 Harrison Street 1879-89
Judge

Lewis, John B.
409 Bryant Street 1869-92
Real Estate

Lincoln, Jerome
18 Laurel Place 1861-67
334 Beale Street 1868-81
555 Harrison Street 1881-1906
Real Estate & Banking

Lindenberger, Thomas E.
549 Folsom Street 1861-62
333 2nd Street 1863-65
345 Beale Street 1866-68
Badger & Lindenberger, Importers

Livermore, Horatio G. and H.P.
Minna between 2nd & 3rd St. 1859
Folsom St. between 2nd & 3rd 1860
Coffin & Redington (Drugs)

Louderback, Davis
545 Folsom 1874-80
Judge (Brother of
Andrew Louderback)

Low, C. Adolphe
741 Howard Street 1862
26 Laurel Place 1864-65
Merchant

Low, Charles Allen
434 2nd Street 1874
Oil Importer
(Son of Charles L. Low)

Low, Charles L.
553 Harrison Street 1863-70
58 South Park 1874-77
Capitalist (brother of
Governor Frederick Low)

Lucas, Robert H.& Robert, Jr.
18 & later 22 & later
33 South Park 1879-82
Ice Company

Lucky, Reverend William T.
32 South Park 1870-71
Principal, State Normal School

Lyle, Joshua B.
Howard Street between
2nd & 3rd 1856-61
Commission Merchant

Lyons, Judge Henry A.
501 Harrison Street 1871
415 1st Street 1872
Capitalist

Lux, Charles
45 South Park 1863-78
Miller & Lux, Cattle ranches

Macondray, Frederick, Jr.
605 Harrison Street 1866-69
Importer, Shipping

Macpherson, Alexander
Beale Street near
Harrison Street 1863-65
1st between Harrison &
Bryant Streets 1867-70
Lumber Mills

Madison, Captain Bennet
25 Frederick Street 1864-71
447 Bryant Street 1876
Shipping; Pres., Marine Exchange

Magill, Robert
19 Stanley Place 1864-70
Insurance

Mann, George
31 South Park 1863-90
Insurance

Marwedel, Charles F.
6 Vassar Place 1860-70
Hardware

Masten, Nathan K.
21 & later 15 South Park 1859-88
Real Estate & Banking

Mathieu, Julian
666 Harrison Street 1863-65
Importer

Maxwell, Mrs. Susan
41 South Park 1866-68
Widow

Maynard, George
410 Harrison Street 1873-74
16 South Park 1875-80
Widow lived at 642
Folsom Street 1880-82
City & County Auditor
(Brother of Lafayette & John)

Maynard, Lafayette
326 2nd Street 1862-66
346 1st Streets 1867-69
557 Harrison Street 1873-77
Real Estate (Grandson was artist,
Lafayette Maynard Dixon)

McAllister, Cutler
417 1st Street 1864-75
Attorney

McAllister, Hall
415 1st Street 1865-71
Attorney
McAllister Street Namesake

McDougal, Charles J.
606 Folsom Street 1874-75
16 South Park 1880-81
Commodore, U.S. Navy

McDougal, David
46 South Park 1876-78
58 South Park 1880-83
Admiral, U.S. Navy

McDougall, General James H.
South Park 1860
U.S. Senator, California

McKibbin, William
East side 2nd Street near
Mission Street 1859-66
later 3rd Street near Mission St.
Iron Works

McKinstry, Elisha W.
44 South Park 1866-77
Justice, Calif. Supreme Court

McLane, Charles
500 Harrison Street 1868-82
Wells, Fargo & Co.

McLane, Louis
438 Bryant Street 1859-61 & 1875-8
President, Wells Fargo Bank

McMahon, Frederick P.
South East corner Tehama &
1st Streets 1859-66
President, Fairhaven Oil

McNevin, Captain Edmund
406 Beale Street 1877-92
Navigation

McRuer, Donald C.
Rincon Place 1856
18 Laurel Place 1859-84
Whale Oil, later Insurance,
U.S. Congressman

Meares, Dr. John L.
428 Bryant 1879
642 Folsom Street 1882
614 Folsom 1886
Physician & Health Officer

Meeks, Washington
31 Hawthorne Street 1867-85
Attorney

Meigs, George
558 Folsom Street 1875-80
Lumber

Mendell, Col. George H.
342 and 420 Fremont Street 1878-88
Engineer, U.S. Army

Merrill, John C.
14 Stanley Place 1856-87
Shipping

Merrill, Oliver
663 Block Harrison Street 1875-88
Capitalist

Meussdorffer, John C.
752 Folsom Street 1862-79
Importer, Hats

Middleton, John
501 2nd Street 1861-62
Real Estate & Assemblyman

Miel, Rev. Charles
41 & later 54-55 South Park 1864-66
Professor, Young Ladies' Institute

Miller, Henry
430 Bryant Street 1872-74
34 Essex Place 1877-06
Cattle King

Mizner, Lansing
337 Beale Street 1859-63
Attorney, U.S. Minister to Guatemala
Father of the "Many Mizners"

Moffat, Eugene
550 Bryant Street 1874-75
Meat

Moffat, Henry
433 Bryant Street 1885 to late 90s
Meat

Monsen, Frederick
523 Folsom Street 1898
14 Stanley Place 1900
21 Stanley Place 1902
Wholesale Photographic Supplies

Moon, Andrew
514 3rd Street 1856-63
Broker, Real Estate

Moore, Alfred S.
24 Hawthorne Street 1868-69
573 Harrison Street 1870-77
Shipping Merchant

Moore, John M.
668 Harrison Street 1864-68
22 Stanley Place 1871-76
Broker

Moore, Joseph
668 Harrison Street 1864-68
Attorney

Moore, Joseph
642 2nd Street 1866-74
213 Harrison Street 1878-85
Risdon Iron Works, President of
Vulcan Foundry, 1860s
Grandfather of Joseph Moore, Jr.

Morgan, James
3rd Street between Folsom &
Harrison Streets 1856-60
Liquor Dealer

Morrison, Andrew L.
440 2nd Street 1862-66
Mining

Mott, Gordon W. & William H.
33 Hawthorne Street 1873-87
Attorney

Moulton, Frank
607 Harrison Street 1870-87
Goodyear Rubber
(Son of Josiah Moulton;
daughter was Mrs. Chas. Merrill)

Moulton, Josiah
209 2nd Street 1859-61
607 Harrison Street 1862-84
Paint Dealer

Myers, John
657 Folsom Street 1869-77
Liquor Dealer

Nagle, George D.
16 Rincon Place 1859-70
Contractor

Nelson, Charles
335 Bryant Street 1859-61
9 Laurel Place 1872
30 Laurel Place 1874-83
Sea Captain

Newbury, Christopher
334 Fremont Street 1872-80
Ship Captain

Newhall, Henry Mayo
334 Beale Street 1854-74
Auctioneer, later Newhall Land Co.

Newhall, William M.
323 Fremont Street 1862-74
Newhall Land Company

Newlands, Francis G.
656 Folsom Street 1881-86
Latham's former home
U.S. Senator, Nevada
(Married U.S. Senator
William Sharons's daughter)

Nickel, Leroy, Sr.
19 Stanley Place 1883
16 Rincon Place 1884-86
Ranching (Miller & Lux)
Married Henry Miller's daughter

Nisbet, James
30 Rincon Place 1862-65,
Editor, Evening Bulletin
Lived with J.C. Hopkins

Norton, George M.
348 Fremont Street 1854-66
Mining

Nugent, John
730 Howard Street 1862
Editor, S.F. Herald

Nugent, Rev. John F.
320 Harrison Street 1882-1890s
Pastor, St. Brendan's Church at
Fremont & Harrison Street

O'Connor, Cornelius
316 Bryant Street 1870-78
Stocks (with Flood & O'Brien)

O'Connor, John F.
69 South Park 1856-59
Importer; Iron & Steel

Ogden, Fred
408 2nd Street 1861
427 2nd Street 1865-68
28 Rincon Place 1872-78
U.S. Quartermasters Warehouse;
later with Richard L. Ogden

Ogden, Captain Richard L.
Essex & Harrison Street 1860
South West corner 2nd &
Harrison Streets 1862-64
435 Bryant Street 1874-76
30 South Park 1877-84
Commission Merchant; later insurance;
& later Kimball Manufacturing Co.

Ortiz, Celedonio
7 South Park 1871-73
16 South Park 1874-76
430 Bryant Street 1877-86
Merchant

Osgood, Charles
South Park 1856
Merchant

Otis, James
26 & later 17 South Park 1859-67
Mayor of San Francisco
(married Lucy, daughter of
Captain Frederick Macondray)

Paddock, Nathan
49 South Park 1970-86
Banker

Page, Dr. Thomas
58 South Park 1871-72
Grandfather, Charles Page
Physician

Palache, Gilbert
321 Fremont Street 1859-86
With Newhall & Company

Palmer, Cyrus
329, later 331 2nd Street 1853-1869
3 Essex Place 1869-73
16 Rincon Place 1874-87
Miner's Foundry

Palmer, Wales
327 2nd Street 1853-68
4 Essex 1870-92
Golden State Iron Works

Palmer, W.A. & later his widow
327 2nd Street 1853-68
2 Essex Street 1870-87
Pacific Foundry, later Golden Gate
Foundry

Park, Trenor
Tehama Street between 2nd &
3rd 1856-59
Attorney

Parrott, John
620 Folsom Street 1854-86
Banker

Payson, Henry R.
Bryant Street between
2nd & 3rd 1856-59
Secretary, Sacramento RR

Pease, Emery T.
37 South Park 1860-74
Stockbroker

Peel, Jonathan
540 Folsom Street 1856-73
Real Estate

Perkin, Samuel
22 Hawthorne Street 1860-84
Lumber

Peterson, Frank & Ferdinand C.
12 Essex Street 1873-86
Canning Co. & Insurance

Pierson, James
Laurel Place 1859-60
Importer

Pinckard, George, M.
7 South Park 1876
618 Harrison Street 1871-80
Transfer Company

Piper, Jerome B.
15 DeBoom Street 1867-89
Piper Line Bay & River Schooners

Pitts, John H.
23 South Park 1877-81
19 South Park 1882-85
Commission Merchant

Platt, George M.
525 Folsom Street 1866-68
Commission Merchant

Plummer Family
(George, William & Others)
62 Tehama Street 1862-81
With Newhall & Company;
& Lumber Dealer

Poett, Alfred C.
416 Harrison Street 1874-75
17 Stanley Place 1877-81
30 Laurel Place 1883-86
Engineer

Pope, A.J.
Vernon Place 1860
614 Folsom 1861-83
Pope & Talbot Lumber

Poultney, George
342-344 Bryant Street 1860-68
330 Brannen 1870-80
South Park Stables

Poulterer, Thomas J.
South Park 1856-60
Auctioneer

Pratt, Orville C.
213 1st Street 1859-68
S.E. corner Harrison &
2nd Street 1870
26 Laurel Place 1871-74
Judge

Ralston, William C.
348 Fremont Street 1862-70
Banker

Rand, William B.
574 Folsom Street 1868-79
Coal & Iron

Rankin, Ira
416 Harrison Street 1862-70
Pacific Foundry,
Customs Collector, Port of S.F.

Raymond, Israel Ward
34 Essex Street 1867-69
406 2nd 1870
Steamship Companies

Redington, John
31 South Park 1856-61
Drugs & Quicksilver Mines

Reinhart, Benjamin
710 Folsom Street 1863-70
Merchant

Reis, Christian
16 South Park 1867-68
Real Estate & Banking

Ringgold, Col. George H.
658 Folsom Street 1860-62
12 Hawthorne Street 1863-65
U.S.Army

Risdon, John N.
213 Harrison Street 1856-68
Risdon Iron Works

Ritchie, Archibald A.
18 South Park 1856
(His widow lived there until 1874)
Sea Captain, Ranch Owner

Roberts, James B.
339 2nd Street 1867-70
572 Harrison Street 1871-92
Importer; Insurance

Robinson, Alfred
26 Essex Street 1879-95
Trustee of Stearn's Ranches

Robinson, Juan
59 South Park 1867-78
Capitalist

Roethe, Christian
461 Bryant Street 1870-85
Druggist

Rogers, Dan
357 Brannan Street 1856-74
Attorney, State Assembly 1860

Rogers, Robert C.
357 Brannan Street 1856-74
Attorney, Real Estate

Rosenfeld, John
307 Folsom Street 1861-66
Coal Dealer

Rothschild, Henry
734 Folsom Street 1866-76
Merchant

Rothwell, W.
1st Street between
Harrison & Bryant Streets 1856
Flour Dealer

Rottanzi, Antonio, M.D.
301 3rd Street 1862-90
Physician & Druggist

Rountree, James O.
423 2nd Street 1859-69
Wholesale Grocer

Rowe, Albert
118 Silver 1859-71
16 Perry 1872-88
Shipwright
(Father of Albert Rowe M.D.,
famous allergist)

Russ, Horace P.
South Park 1859
President, Quartz Mining Assoc.

Sanderson, Judge Silas W.
17 South Park 1871
Chief Justice, Calif. Supreme Court
(Father of Sibyl Sanderson,
famous opera singer)

Sather, Peder
N.W. Corner Harrison Street &
2nd Street 1856-71
Banker

Savage, Richard
403 Bryant Street 1868-69
Iron Works, Empire Foundry

Sawtelle, General C.G.
406 Bryant Street 1870
U.S. Army

Sawyer, William B.
2nd Street between
Folsom & Harrison Streets 1856
Paints

Scales, William
Harrison Street between
Fremont and Beale 1856
Agent, Santa Clara Flour Mills

Scholle, William, Jacob, and Abraham
642 Folsom 1862-77
Grain Dealers

Scott, Albert W.
Beale Street 1859
225 Harrison Street 1861-68
19 Rincon Place 1869-85
Hay & Grain, School Director

Scott, Henry T.
507 Harrison Street 1874-75
Union Iron Works

Scott, Irving M.
507 Harrison Street 1874-06
Union Iron Works

Scott, Reverend William A.
South Park 1856
332 2nd Street 1859-61
Presbyterian Minister

Scudder, Reverend Henry
1 Vernon Place 1866-70
Pastor, Howard Presby. Church

Selby, Thomas H. & family
618 Harrison Street 1854-79
S. F. Mayor & Selby Smelting Co.

Sesnon, William T.
646 Folsom Street 1882-84
Attorney's Office

Shaffer, Oscar L.
13 Tehama Street 1856-61
337 Beale Street 1862
Judge

Shaw, Henry B.
254 2nd Street 1868-73
Druggist

Sheldon, John P.
655 Harrison Street 1875-80
Lumber

Shepherd, John L.
W.Side Hawthorne Street 1859-61
San Francisco Chemical Works

Sherburne, Col. John P.
475 Bryant Street 1867-69
504 3rd Street 1870
Adjutant General's Office

Sherman, Charles H.
South side Bryant Street
near 2nd 1856-61
Carpets, later Jewelry

Sherman, John H.
657 Howard Street 1864-65
Physician

Sherman, Gen. William Tecumseh
410 Harrison Street 1855-57
U.S.Army; San Francisco Banker

Sherwood, Robert
433 Bryant Street 1965-81
Jeweler

Shrader, Andrew J.
441 Brannan Street 1862-69
5 South Park 1870-90's
Wholesale Butcher, S.F. Supervisor
Shrader Street namesake

Shreve, George C.
528 Harrison Street 1860-61
412 2nd Street 1862-68
Jeweler

Sielken, John H.
23, later 58 South Park 1877-82
Commission Merchant

Sinton, Richard H.
16 South Park 1867-71
Commssion Merchant

Smedberg, Col. William, R.
24 Essex Street 1868-69
412 2nd Street 1870
U.S.Army

Smith, Frederick
28 South Park 1859-63
Importer

Smith, George W.
225 Harrison Streets 1856-62
Contractor

Smith, Sidney M.
28 South Park 1859-61
328 Bryant Street 1862-90s
Canning

Smith, D. Sidney
South side Harrison, between
Fremont & Beale Streets 1856
Rincon Place 1859-61
Merchant

Smith, Sidney
Laurel Place 1856-59
Attorney

Smith, William M.
341 Bryant Street 1883-88
7 South Park 1889-97
Sea Captain

Sneath, Richard G.
646 Folsom Street 1856-68
Importer; later
prominent in San Mateo County

Somers, Don Carlos
444 2nd Street 1861-64
401 Bryant Street 1870-75
Grocer (Chrysopolis Market)

Soule, Samuel & Philander
323 1st Street 1867-1892
Lumber

Spotts, James H.
19 South Park 1875-80
Commodore, U.S. Navy

Stanford, A.P.
46 South Park 1856-65
Stanford Brothers, Oil Importers
(brother of Leland)

Starr, Thomas
506 3rd Street 1863-65
Golden State Bakery

Stevens, Levi
4 Essex Street 1862-76
President, Merchants Exchange Bank

Stevens, Captain William W.
153 Natoma Street 1861-65
Sea Captain

Stoddard, Charles Warren
3 Vernon Place 1879-82
(Sather's old house)
42 Hawthorne Street 1883-84
Author, Poet

Stoddard, David
313 Fremont Street 1873-75
Engineer

Story, Charles R.
447 Bryant Street 1862-66
Tax Collector

Story, George L.
412 2nd Street 1860-62
Importer, Prints

Stow, Joseph W.
309 Harrison Street 1863-65
530 Harrison Street 1866-69
Hardware

Swain, Josiah W.
314 Fremont Street 1865-69
Bay City Livery Stables

Symmes, Frank J.
628 Harrison Street 1872-76
(Thomas Day's home)
Thomas Day & Co.

Talbot, William C.
610 Folsom Street 1859-72
Pope & Talbot Lumber

Taylor, Edward & William
336 2nd Street 1860-66
Pacific Mail Steamship Co.

Taylor, John B.
Clementina Street,
near 2nd Street 1859-60
229 1st Street 1861-65
Produce Dealer

Tevis, Lloyd
South Park 1859
President, Wells, Fargo & Co.

Tewsbury, Jacob
N.E. corner South Park &
519 3rd Street 1867-73
Physician, Real Estate

Thompson, Smith B.
373 Brannan Street 1866-70
Builder & School Director

Tichenor, Henry B.
433 2nd Street 1866-68
427 2nd Street 1868-88
Lumber & River Packets

Tingley, Col. George B.
& later his widow
27 Hawthorne Street 1862-90
Attorney

Tilden, Joseph
641 Harrison Street 1873-74
434 2nd Street 1875-79
30 Hawthone Street 1880-85
Chairman, Pacific Stock Exchange
(Famous early Bohemian Club member)

Todd, Alexander H.
2nd Street, between Harrison &
Bryant Streets 1856
Broker

Todd, John
Beale Street, between Harrison &
Bryant Streets 1864-66
Boots & Shoes

Townsend, Judge James
346 Beale Street 1859-64
Judge

Tubbs, Alfred L.
349 Fremont Street 1863-80
(Stanford's Old Home)
Tubbs Cordage

Tucker, John
N.W. corner Harrison &
Essex Streets 1860-65
Jeweler

Turk, Frank
Folsom Street, between
2nd & 3rd Streets 1852
Attorney, Town Council

Twiggs, John W.
655 Harrison Street 1878-80
Assayer

Urmy, John B.
41 Clementina Street 1861-62
Publisher
Father of poet Clarence Urmy

Uznay, Charles
North side Harrison Street,
between 2nd & 3rd Streets 1856-60
419 Bryant Street 1863-65
Calif. Metallurgical Works

Van Bergen, John & Nicholas
545 Folsom Street 1861-65
Importer

Van Slicklen, Frederick C.
47 South Park 1880-85
Commission Merchant

Vassault, Ferdinand
3 Vernon Place 1863-65
37 South Park 1866-69
Real Estate

Von Schmidt, Alexander W.
Hawthorne Street 1856
South Park 1859
530 Harrison Street 1860-61
Guy Place 1862-65
Engineer & Spring Valley Water

Von Schroeder, Baron John Henr
553 Harrison Street 1886-90
(Son-in-law of Peter Donahue)

Wakelee, Henry P.
311 Harrison Street 1859-66
Drugs

Wakeman. Alonzo & later his wid
51 Tehama Street,
between 1st & 2nd Streets 1859-76
U.S. Quartermaster Dept.

Wakeman, Captain F.O.
Pleasant Valley 1852-59
Land Agent

Wallace, George
29 South Park 1859-61
Secretary to Governor Downey

Walter, Theodore V.
40 South Park 1874-79
Banker

Walton, N.C.
East side Essex Place 1856
Liquor Merchant

Wandesforde, Juan B.
10 De Boom Street 1862-72
Artist

Ward, George R.
South side Laurel Place 1856
Broker

Washburn, E.H.
West side 2nd Street,
near Harrison Street 1859
Auctioneer

Washington, Col. Benjamin
440 Bryant Street 1859-62
Collector, Port of San Francisco

Watkins, Commodore James T.
58 South Park 1859-68
Ship Captain, Pacific Mail S.S. Co.

Weber, Adolph C.
840 Folsom Street 1859-90
President, Humboldt Bank
Brother of Capt. Charles Weber
of Stockton (House still standing
in Santa Cruz Mountains)

Webster, Frank E.
Laurel Place, 1860
62 Stanley Place 1861-66
Streamship Lines

Weletsky, Vlademir
33 & 7 South Park 1876-81
Consul General to Russia

Wellman, Bela
516 3rd Street 1863-64
350 1st Street 1864-68
Wellman Peck, Grocers

Wells, Robert
Harrison Street,
between 1st & 2nd Streets 1856-59
Bay City Brewery

Wheaton, George H.
3 Vernon Place 1867-68
518 Howard Street 1868-69
530 Harrison Street 1870-73
Commission Merchant

Wheeler, Alfred
403 Bryant Street 1866-77
343 Bryant Street 1877-81
Attorney

Wheeler, John O.
37 South Park 1871-72
433 Second Street 1873-74
Chief Clerk, Indian Affairs

White, William A.
Beale Street, between Folsom &
Harrison Streets 1856-59
325 Fremont Street 1860-88
With Newhall Co.

Whiting, Richard L.
South Park 1856-59
Ship Captain

Whittier, W. Frank
528 Howard Street 1861-66
Paints, later with Fuller

Wickman, William & later his widow
21 Essex Street 1860-68
Ship Chandlers

Wiegard, Conrad
1st Street, between
Folsom & Harrison Streets 1856
Assayer, U.S. Mint

Wieland, John
228 2nd Street 1858-89
President, Philadelphia Brewing Co.

Wiggins, Wilfred W.
403 Bryant Street 1860-62
46 South Park 1863-73
Attorney & Banker

Wigmore, John
N. Side Tehama Street,
between 2nd & 3rd Streets 1860-64
Cabinet Maker; later Lumber Dealer,
Father of John Wigmore
(Wigmore on Evidence)

Wildes, Joseph
448 Second Street 1864-65
359 Bryant Street 1866-71
628 Harrison Street 1872-85
U.S. Surveyor

Williams, George A. & George S.
616 Harrison Street 1872-88
4 Vernon Place 1889-92
With Selby & Co.

Williams, George E.
226 2nd Street 1867-76
Grandfather of Dwight Clarke

Williams, Henry B.
416 Harrison Street 1874
27 South Park 1878
319 1st 1880-90
Williams, Dimond & Co.

Wilson, Charles L.
E. Side 2nd Street 1859
345 Fremont Street 1861
Contractor

Wilson, Cyrus
Stanley Place 1856-60

Wilson, George O.
328 Fremont Street 1863-64
490 First Street 1862
Wilson Brothers, Doors, Windows

Wilson, N. Irving
415 Harrison Street 1859-62
320 Fremont Street 1864-65
341 Fremont Street 1866
Wilson Brothers Doors, Windows

Wilson, John
552 Folsom Street 1867-77
Paints & Oils

Wilson, General John O.
402 Fremont Street 1854-77
Attorney

Winall, Stuart A.
311 Fremont Street 1859-65
Carriage Makers

Winans, John
573 Harrison Street 1864-66
24 South Park 1867-69
553 Harrison Street 1871-74
Stockbroker

Woods, I.C.
420 2nd Street 1871-72
Manufacturing
(formerly Adams Express)

Woodward, Robert B.
South Park, corner of
3rd Street 1859-60
Woodward's Gardens

Woodworth, Selim & Frederick
Minna Street 1856-59
32 Hawthorne Street 1860-61
Importer

Wozencraft, Oliver M.
43 South Park 1862-65
Physician

Wyman, Captain Benjamin Henry
315 2nd Street 1861
(Octogon House of Palmer)
Purser, Pacific Mail S.S. Co.
(Married sister of Bret Harte)

Yale, Gregory
35 South Park 1860-70
Mining Attorney

Zeitska, Bertha
51-55 South Park 1867-77
President, Young Ladies' Institute

INDEX